"I have a tremendous amount of respect for Marsh as a person and as a radio and TV personality. He's tops in both respects. He's very accurate and wears so well. This is a book that all of Marsh's fans from Duluth and Iron Range will enjoy and the entire WCHA listening audience, as well."

**Paul Giel, former Athletic Director, University of Minnesota**

"The book is Marsh all the way. He is an honest, easy to have around type of person. It's enjoyable to remember times gone by, since we were in the same era of life and sports. Names were vey familiar to me throughout the book. *Marsh* is a very deserving story that was worth recording for history."

**Jim Malosky, UMD football coach**

"In all of my 40 years as a coach and athletic director, I've never met a more personable leader of sports, more knowledgeable man of sports, a more cooperative person than Marsh Nelson."

**Mertz Mortorelli, former Men's Athletic Director, UWS**
**From a letter dated April 30, 1984**

"Marsh Nelson is probably the most recognizable sports personality in the Northland—right up there with Bud Grant, Kevin McHale and Brett Hull. *Marsh* is a rare combination of words and subject material that makes for enjoyable reading. Author Don Wright has woven a warm tale of a small town boy who grew to leave an indelible imprint on regional sports."

**Bruce Bennett, Associate Sports Editor**
**Duluth News-Tribune**

"What makes Marsh a favorite of mine in broadcasting is trust. I've known him for years as a friend and for almost as many years as a broadcast personality. I've found him honest and open, a person of understanding and curiosity. . . . this study of Marsh conveys that. . . . I recommend it."

**Jim Klobuchar, Star Tribune, Minneapolis**

# MARSH

## a lifetime
## in
## *Sports!*

**by Don Wright**

*Best Wishes,*
*Sue - and*
*for many more*
*Victories!.*

*Marsh Nelson*

Pfeifer-Hamilton

Pfeifer-Hamilton Publishers
1702 E Jefferson St
Duluth MN 55812 (218) 728-6807

**MARSH**
a lifetime in sports

Printed in the United States of America by Versa Press Inc
10 9 8 7 6 5 4 3 2 1

Larry Fortner, Senior Editor
Tina P Olson, Project Director
Joy Morgan Dey, Book Designer

Library of Congress Cataloging in Publication Data
91-60892


ISBN 0-938586-46-7

*To Judy and Margaret,*
*who never doubted.*

# CONTENTS

# Introduction

J ohn Russell Snee settles into the only chair in the disorder of Marsh Nelson's tiny office in Broadcast Center. Phone booths in this world are larger than Marsh's office. His only window looks into the television newsroom, which Marsh calls the "Madhouse." The sun never shines on his cluttered desk.

The usual small talk passes quickly between two friends who share the experience of many years behind a broadcast microphone. For a long moment John eyes the nameplate teetering on the edge of the scarred desk. The nameplate bears the single word "Nelson"— superfluous identification for a man whose face and voice are as familiar as scrambled eggs and bacon in thousands of households across three states.

Snee, general manager of Duluth's KDAL Radio, has not come to reminisce. He looks across the desk at the ruddy face topped with a shock of straight, sandy hair. The erstwhile crewcut is gone. Today, Marsh Nelson's face has a few more lines, but they fail to hide the little-boy enthusiasm and eagerness that have marked a generation in sports as participant, observer and commentator.

"Marsh, would you feel bad if you weren't doing hockey on radio anymore?" Snee's question is blunt, unexpected.

Suddenly 27 years of broadcasting college hockey flash by in a panorama of memories: the old Duluth Curling Club . . . a skidding car crash . . . a light plane's forced landing on a dark, snowy highway . . . shared toilet facilities with the vice president of the United States . . . the gamy smell of the Denver Coliseum after a cattle show . . . the "Doghouse" in Houghton, Michigan, with its coiled rope for a fire escape . . . the "Potato Barn" in Grand Forks . . . faulty broadcast phone lines . . . long, lonely winter drives . . . the ad libs . . . the interviews . . . the friends and competitors whose voices are now stilled in death.

Thirty-nine years ago Marshall Leonard Nelson first spoke into a live mike. Broadcasting has been his life ever since: more than a quarter-century as the stadium voice of the Minnesota Vikings, 34 consecutive years in sports broadcasting—33 of them on the same Duluth television station, perhaps an unequaled record of longevity in an industry known for its revolving-door personnel turnovers. Snee's question hangs in the air, unanswered: "Would you feel bad . . . ?"

It was a question long in coming, but when it came it still was a shock. The promos used to say, "Nobody calls 'em better than Marsh." He'd been sports director of both KDAL Radio and Television in Duluth since January 1, 1958. Following the separate sales of the radio and TV stations several years ago, Marsh became employed exclusively by the television station, its call letters changed to KDLH-TV. For special events, notably University of Minnesota-Duluth hockey play-by-play, KDAL purchased his services from the TV station—until that summer day in 1988 when the radio station hierarchy made a strictly dollars-and-cents decision.

"I probably would have quit the hockey on my own if they hadn't done it for me," Marsh says, months later. "I just don't know when. I wanted to be the one to make the final decision, rather than have somebody tell me they don't want me anymore because they can save x-dollars by having a radio staffer broadcast hockey instead of me."

He looks around the office cubicle, its walls covered with memorabilia: pennants, buttons, badges, posters, snapshots, ribbons, certificates and awards . . . testimonials to a lifetime in sports broadcasting and service to youth athletics.

"When you've been doing something for this long, you wonder how you'll react when you're no longer doing it. My first reaction was relief, and experience has taught me that your first reaction is right. Instinct never lets you down.

"If you're in this business long enough, you get the idea they can't get along without you. They can. As soon as you walk out the door somebody else walks in. Nobody's indispensable."

Marsh shifts in his chair. Off the air his voice is noticeably lower, relaxed, in contrast to his broadcast delivery.

"As I was getting up into 23 and 24 years with the hockey remotes, I realized I wouldn't be doing it forever. I used to think when I stopped it would be the end of the world. It's not.

"The seasons seemed longer and longer. Over the years, it begins to wear on you, the road trips. You leave on Thursday and come back home on Sunday, dragging suitcases and a couple of sacks of equipment across one airport after another, worrying about whether the phone lines are in, whether the batteries are dead or the mikes are going to work, or whether somebody's taking care of the scores back at the station.

"Why do you do it? You do it because you love it. No other reason. It certainly isn't the money. The money's not that great. If you love this business, you put up with the problems."

He smiles and shakes his head. The large brown eyes twinkle.

"For instance, at Tully Forum in Lowell [Massachusetts], there was a little spring missing in our equipment, and the phone connection for the broadcast was so bad I had to jam a matchstick into the terminal to hold the wires tight. That matchstick kept me on the air for two and a half hours. A matchstick! I don't even smoke! Quit when I was in eighth grade."

He pauses, picks up a pencil and idly circles the current date on a large calendar pad among the sports schedules, script pages, notes, photos, video cassettes and audio tapes that litter his desk. After a long moment he continues.

"I don't think it's any different than, say, the grader operator out there who works on the highway. He has pride in what he's doing. When they tell him he can't run the grader anymore he walks away from it with a sense of loss. I feel the same way about not broadcasting hockey.

"Sure, I miss some of the things connected with doing the games, most of all the players, the coaches. I miss being with those guys—Terry Shercliffe, Mike Sertich, Bill Selman, Ralph Romano, Gus Hendrickson—winning and losing with them. And I miss the people, the camaraderie of the hockey fans. But they're still my friends and they always will be."

Marsh Nelson's friends number in the hundreds, the thousands, but, he's never met most of them. They know his voice and his face. They invite him into their homes twice a day, five days a week, at supper time and just before bedtime. They feel that surely he knows them; they forget the one-way vision of the television camera. Marsh walks down Superior Street in Duluth—or Hennepin Avenue in Minneapolis, or Kellogg Boulevard in downtown St. Paul, or Tower Avenue in Superior, or Main Street anywhere in Northern Minnesota, Wisconsin or Michigan—and people greet him like a personal friend. They reach out to slap his back or touch his arm.

"Hey, Marsh!" youngsters yell from across the street. They're rewarded with a grin, a wave and a "How are ya, pal!" In spidery handwriting, Marsh signs autographs with the frequency of a

Hollywood star, all the while wondering in awe at his own celebrity status, and loving every minute of the attention.

"Sure, it's embarassing sometimes. But I'd be more embarassed if they didn't recognize me. I'm just a hick from Tower, Minnesota. If I've been successful over the years, maybe it's because I've been around for so darn long." He apparently is unaware that the reverse could also be true.

The idea for this book was born in a dinner conversation one evening with Marsh and his wife, Judy, reliving and laughing about experiences Marsh and I have had during many years in broadcasting. Judy was a believer in the book then and all through the long weeks and months that followed. Marsh's initial reluctance ("Who'd want to read a book about me?") gradually changed to enthusiastic participation. I consider it to be the best idea I ever had.

A few people deserve special thanks for helping along the way. First and foremost is Judy Nelson for inspiration, encouragement and unflagging support; for providing a blazing fireplace, innumerable pots of coffee, fine wine, dinners, lunches and snack treats—and for helping to draw out the real Marsh Nelson from a sometimes reticent husband.

Thanks, too, to all who contributed time, stories and remembrances, especially KDLH-TV's Mary Jo White, former News Director Ron Lund and former engineer-cameraman C. Bruce Nimmo; KDAL Radio Program Director Rik Jordan; Donn Larson, an early production supervisor at KDAL-TV; Ray Peil, Warren Kregness and Herb Lamppa, all of Tower; "JoJo" Vatalaro; Don Avikainen of Silver Bay; Earl Henton, my friend of many years and veteran of microphone and camera; KDLH-TV for pictures; Marsh's daughter Ginger; former Duluth Dukes business manager and long-time Morgan Park High School coach Graydon "Soup" Stromme; Associate Sports Editor Bruce Bennett for proofing and for permission to quote from his *Duluth*

*News-Tribune* column; and to those few patient souls who read and re-read early drafts of the manuscript and offered suggestions and encouragement, especially Margaret Gates, my son Steve, my daughter Amy and particularly writer/historian Bill Beck—a literary agent whose rates are right. To my publisher, Don Tubesing, and my editor, Larry Fortner, a hearty thanks for one of the best Christmas presents I ever had.

This is not a sports book, although love of sports is the theme. This is not a book about athletes, although they people its pages. This is not a behind-the-scenes peek at radio and television, although that's the setting for most of the story. Finally, this is not an unbiased and objective account—because it's about a friend, by a friend.

Don Wright
Duluth, Minnesota

CHAPTER ONE

# Long Shot

The blond crewcut kid with the broad grin and wide-eyed stare shifted his weight on the bench and extended his right leg to rub his knee gently, easing the nagging pain that persisted from the basketball injury he'd suffered a month ago back home. He hid the knee brace and tried to ignore the discomfort. It wouldn't do to let anyone know about the injury. Too much was at stake. Anyway, he told himself, it hardly bothered him. After all, it wasn't every week you had a tryout with the New York Giants.

His eyes swept the field, one of eight baseball diamonds the Giants were using this day in Sanford, Florida. It was February 1949, and he'd been here nearly two weeks. He'd graduated from high school two years before. His two-week vacation from his Minnesota Highway Department job was almost used up. Another day and Marsh Nelson would have to get back on the bus and go home.

The hometown folks thought he was major league material. True, he lacked a lot of skills, but the Iron Rangers who'd seen

1

him play insisted "the pros can teach you the things you need to know if you have reasonable native ability."

But even in those days it wasn't easy to break into the majors. There were only eight teams each in the American and National leagues, and there was nothing like today's extensive scouting program.

Marsh brushed at a smudge of dirt on the front of his Ely BluSox shirt. He'd written to the Giants a couple of months earlier and sent some statistics from his city team baseball games. The Giants hadn't promised a thing when they told him to come on down—at his own expense.

"I got on the bus at Tower at 5 o'clock on a Friday afternoon and, except for changes at Duluth and Indianapolis, and the meal stops, I stayed on that bus 'til I got to Sanford Monday morning at 6:30. I wasn't much more than a walk-in off the street."

The odds seemed awesome. He was one of about 750 hopefuls at the Giants' spring tryout camp. The players were divided into eight teams and worked every day for five hours.

He'd felt a little self-conscious about the Ely baseball shirt when he reported in. "Nobody knows me from a bale of hay," he thought. But the shirt proved to be an asset when he was assigned to the unit coached by Tom Sheehan, then manager of the Minneapolis Millers, the Giants' No. 1 farm team. Sheehan knew about Ely and spent a little extra time with Marsh.

At the same time, the Giants were considering another rookie, a youngster from the Birmingham Black Barons. His name was Willie Mays.

Marsh watched intently as Giants slugger Bobby Thomson shagged fly balls in the outfield. "They had one of those compressed-air guns that shoot baseballs for batting practice, and they'd figured out how to aim it straight up for flys. The ball almost went out of sight," he recalls. Warming the bench on the edge of the field, watching Thomson and others work, even the eternal optimist that lives inside Marsh Nelson knew that signing with the Giants was a remote possibility for a kid from Tower, Minnesota.

Tower is a one-main-street town like dozens of others sprinkled along a line across the Mesabi Range, the sub-surface ore body that snakes 100 miles southwest to northeast across northern Minnesota. Tower was named for Charlemagne Tower, an early railroad and mining entrepreneur. Today Tower is linked by a hyphen and two miles of blacktop highway to its neighbor, Soudan. Together, the two Vermilion Range towns shared the glory of having the state's first, deepest and richest underground iron mine.

Today the mine is silent. Millions of tons of high-grade iron ore—blue Bessemer hematite—still lie undisturbed at the bottom of the deep caverns that once were the Soudan mine, but nobody works the stopes anymore. Now the mine is a state park, the only one in the world where a tourist can drop a half-mile down a mine shaft—the original—in a rattling elevator cage just like the one that once carried hard-rock miners like Charlie Nelson to work.

Charlie Nelson was a diamond driller, a skilled miner who made good wages. It was hard work, the kind that leaves a worker with ringing ears and bone-weary muscles at the end of the day.

Charlie hadn't always been a miner. He was 15 when he came to America from Sweden in 1902 with a third-grade education and a hope for something better. He found it in Tower where his father, John Nelson, and Charlie's older brother, Fred, had stayed temporarily before drifting west to Virginia, Minnesota, 26 miles away.

Tower, Soudan and close-by Ely were bustling, booming, raw young towns. The mines were working, timber was plentiful and times were good. The work was hard and so was the play: saloons at every corner for those who liked their fun loud, noisy and often violent; skating on frozen lakes in winter; hunting in the fall; walks, fishing, baseball, dancing to home-grown music; and dipping *booyah*—a thick beef- vegetable soup—from bubbling cauldrons at the Old Settlers picnic in Lake Vermilion's McKinley Park every summer.

Charlie found lodging with Frank and Lena Sjoberg on East Second Street and soon became good friends with the Sjoberg's young daughter, Hazel.

His job at the sawmill was not exciting, and when an opportunity came with the E. J. Longyear Company as an exploration driller, he seized it. His new job offered more money, a chance to travel and taught him a new skill that was sure to prove useful in a region that depended on iron ore mining.

When war came in 1917, Charlie signed up with the Ninth Infantry Division and served in France with the 346th Field Artillery. When it was over, he, like many young men who marched off to Mr. Wilson's war, went home to many changes. First, he'd lost his innate shyness with women. Second, Hazel Sjoberg had grown up.

Now Hazel was 22 with a trim figure, cascading chestnut hair and flashing, devastating, brown eyes. Charlie Nelson, ex-soldier and driller with Longyear, was entranced.

Today, at 95, Hazel remembers: "I had another boyfriend at the time. He was wonderful. He took me to dances and to parties in Virginia. He and Charlie didn't like each other very much."

Charlie was patient and persistent. The dates became more frequent. Finally he asked Hazel to marry him. "He said if I didn't, he would go to Africa with Longyear," she recalls. "I saved him from that."

They were married in October 1925. Hazel was 29, Charlie 38. Four years later, on September 13, 1929, their only child was born in their two-story white frame house on North Third Street.

The boy's name was Marshall Leonard. . . .

"Nelson! Hey, you . . . Nelson! Get in there again, and try to get it right this time!" Sheehan's bellow jarred the kid's thoughts back to Florida. Marsh jammed his Ely cap on the crewcut and loped toward the infield, the knee forgotten. Marsh felt lucky. Of the 80 or so hopefuls assigned to Sheehan's field, he was playing shortstop in the starting infield.

But his was to be a short career. At the end of the day, Marsh walked over to Sheehan and said goodbye. "Thanks, Coach. I'd like to stay, but I gotta get back to my job."

It was a decision he'd always regret. Sheehan told him to come back next year when, because of Marsh's size, Sheehan would try Marsh either as a catcher or as an outfielder. Marsh never went back.

"I was always a little sorry I didn't pursue it. A lot of baseball people I respect thought I had the right temperament and attitude for a professional ballplayer. Even now, I can't help wondering what would have happened if I'd gone back."

# CHAPTER TWO

# Big Train

Although sports would later become his profession—bordering on obsession—it was not Marsh Nelson's first love.

"Early on, I was fascinated by trains. When I was four or five years old, I had visions of being a locomotive engineer. Tower was right on the railroad, and I'd go down to the station nearly every day to watch the trains come in. I even got to know most of the engineers."

He usually missed the first train of the day, at about 6 a.m., "but I'd be there when the noon passenger went through on the way to Ely, and I'd meet it again when it came back at 2:30. Then, about 5 in the afternoon, when the freight would come from Ely to pick up boxcars and flatcars down at the box factory, I'd be there, too."

As he was to do later in life with sports statistics and the performances of athletes, Marsh committed the train schedules to memory.

"The thirteen-hundreds were the freights, the eleven-hundreds were the passenger trains—1107, 1108, 1109. I even got so I could tell by the whistle in the distance whether it was a passenger or freight.

"I was too little to go alone. Dad was working, of course, and Mom was busy in the kitchen, so Grandpa was elected to take me down to the station two or three times every day."

From time to time, Marsh's grandfather—Charlie's father, John—lived with the Nelsons in their home on Third Street, and there were moments when Grandpa may have regretted the arrangement.

"Sometimes he didn't move as fast as I thought he should," Marsh remembers with some regret. "When I heard the whistle at Tower Junction I was afraid we wouldn't get to the station in time, so I'd give Grandpa a little rap in the shins with my foot and say, 'Let's go, Grandpa! We'll be late!' There are people today who remember me kicking Grandpa in the shins to hurry him up. We were usually on time."

Marsh refutes the local lore that this early fascination for railroading earned him a later nickname: Big Train.

"It was back in the days, just after high school, when I started playing baseball for the Tower Colts. I'd been playing second base for Ely for three years, but when Tower entered the new Mesabi League in 1951 I felt an obligation to go with the home town. That's where I got that nickname.

"We were just getting organized. In fact, Herbie Lamppa and I were the pitching staff. I didn't have much style, no crafty curves, sliders or sinkers. I figured if I just threw the ball hard enough and got it over the plate, I'd be OK. Many years earlier, Walter Johnson, who pitched for the Washington Senators, had the same theory: just throw the ball past the hitter. They called him 'Big Train.'

"Among our fans was a guy named Gawboy. He and his little son never missed a game. When I'd meet 'em downtown, this little guy would yell out: 'Big Train! Big Train!' The name just stuck. It was my pitching, not trains, that got me the name."

On the fringe of Northern Minnesota's wilderness, Tower was made to order for kids who loved the outdoors. The town offered freedom and fresh air, lakes, streams, forest trails and the small town camaraderie that bonds a group of youngsters for life.

"You made your own fun in Tower in the '30s and '40s," Marsh recalls. "We never had any big city recreation department to provide structured activities, but we never seemed to suffer. We were always busy with something."

On hot summer days the gathering place was Dave Anderson's Phillips 66 station on Main Street.

"The guys would drift in there one or two at a time," Marsh says, trying to remember names 50 years later. "Dave's son Bernie, the Bergs, Denny Jackson, Jim Stefanich, Buddy Peterson, Ernie Mustonen, Norm Bruneau. We'd decide then what we'd do that day: go to the playground for a ballgame, or head for the woods to play rubber guns or to Hoodoo Point on Lake Vermilion to swim or smoke, or just get on our bikes and go somewhere, anywhere."

A couple of times a year, the activity turned to petty nocturnal larceny.

"We must have been 10 or 12 years old. We'd wait 'til dark and then swipe vegetables from different gardens, get a chicken and make chicken *booyah* out in the woods. We were very particular about whose garden we robbed; we never stole from relatives, and we never took much."

The story startled Marsh's wife, Judy. "You mean you stole live chickens?"

"Sure. Everybody had chickens. Nobody'd miss a couple once or twice a year. We'd kill and pluck the chicken and toss everything into the pot—breasts, legs, thighs—along with the stolen carrots, celery, cabbage and potatoes, cook it over an open fire for about six hours and have a heck of a *booyah!*"

"Why don't you do that now, at home?" Judy asks.

"It's no fun at home . . . no wild chickens!"

And fun was the ever-present objective.

"There were always three important days when I was growing up. First was opening of fishing season, at that time May 15th. Second was Fourth of July with ballgames, an Indian powwow, sawdust scrambles for quarters and the big parade. Christmas and my birthday tied for third-place importance."

Every spring Marsh and Don Avikainen would rush the fishing season by about three weeks. "Avi and I would have the first walleye feed in town. We'd catch 'em under the bridge by the brewery on the East Two River where the fish would spawn. They were so bountiful we'd scoop 'em out with our hands. One of us would stand on the bridge and watch for the game warden while the other caught fish. I'd take mine home and Mom would fix 'em. She was probably an accomplice after the fact, although she never asked where they came from. Dad knew. He ate 'em anyway."

Fishing filled many summer days.

"I had some secret spots that only a few close friends knew about," Marsh recalls wistfully. "One was out south of town where I'd go for brook trout. On the way, I'd walk past Two-Bit Shorty's shack, and he'd always come out to talk. His real name was Charles Knapp, a little guy, one of the renowned loggers in the area. I'll never forget his advice: 'Always beware of the woman in red.' I'd say, 'Why's that, Two-Bit?' He'd say, 'Why, she had a red dress on, the one who squealed on Dillinger!' Likable little guy—everybody knew Two-Bit." Marsh still attracts characters as friends.

The people of small towns like Tower look forward to any

diversion from the daily routine, and the annual arrival of tent shows, carnivals and circuses were major events.

"I remember one year when the carnival came to town. One of the stands had a so-called game of skill—two empty Coca-Cola bottles standing upside down, side by side. The idea was to knock 'em both down with a tennis ball. It looks easy. The spacing was such that you'd always hit one bottle a split second before the other. One would go over, the other wouldn't. I got so frustrated, dime after dime, trying to get a Kewpie doll, that I went to the drugstore and said to my old friend Walt Martilla, 'Give me a couple of empty Coke bottles, I gotta practice something.'

"After about 10 minutes in the alley, I finally figured out by accident how the game works: if you hit one bottle on the outside, it falls against the other and they both go down. Simple. I went back down to the carnival and cleaned 'em out of Kewpie dolls in about 15 minutes. The man at that stand was glad to get rid of me!"

Each year Halloween required careful planning for pranks befitting the occasion. In the Tower of the 1930s and '40s, indoor plumbing was a rarity, and nearly every family had an outhouse in the backyard. The little utilitarian buildings were prime Halloween targets.

"For ours," Marsh recalls, "Dad put cedar posts down six feet in the ground for bracing. Kids loved to tip over outhouses, but nobody ever tipped ours over. It was too well braced."

He chuckles. "The night before Halloween was 'Gate Night,' when we'd take somebody's gate from one end of town and leave it somewhere on the other end. We'd also move trailers around town. We didn't damage them, just moved 'em around a little from, say, Third Street North to Second Street South—put 'em in a vacant lot or somebody's back yard.

"Policemen were especially vigilant on Gate Night, so we used various diversionary tactics—firecrackers or water bags—to get their attention at one end of town while we were up to some devilment at the other."

Marsh remembers one Halloween prank with a tinge of pride: putting a four-wheel trailer inside the high school, using strategy, tactics and logistics that rivaled an intricate military operation. Timing had to be precise because Marsh's uncle, Elmer Gustafson, was the school janitor.

"We reconnoitered first to find out when Uncle Elmer and the janitors were having coffee in their room in the basement. I'm not sure all the effort was worth it, because the trailer barely fit through the double doors, but we got it in, up the stairs and parked it in front of the office."

Like nearly every small-town kid, Marsh eventually had a paper route, starting with a Virginia weekly, the *Range Facts* or, as he called it, the *Strange Facts*.

"I had that job for about three years, 'til Claude Carlon graduated from high school and I inherited his *Duluth Herald* route. My supervisor was Joe Vidmar from Eveleth, a great guy. He'd come to collect once a week, and Mom would always have cookies or donuts and coffee for him. He loved to come to our house."

A Minneapolis radio station helped keep some of Marsh's deliveries on time.

"I had about 95 daily *Heralds* and, on Sunday, there'd be 50 or 60 thick *News-Tribunes*. The dailies would get to Tower about four o'clock in the afternoon. I'd start the route, but I'd be back at my house a little after five so I could listen to Jack Horner's Sports Corner on KSTP. Then, I'd peddle the 15 papers that were left. I remember some of those customers saying, 'That kid is so prompt you can set your watch by him.' Jack Horner should get the credit."

Marsh Nelson, who would later spend a lifetime in broadcasting, recognizes the changes the industry has wrought in America's values and lifestyle, beginning with his own childhood.

"When we were growing up, nobody imagined anything like television. Radio was new, and many people in Tower didn't even have a radio. Television came along and changed a lot of things forever. First of all, it wiped out the small-town movie theaters that once were institutions around the country."

The Rex Theater in Tower was one of the casualties. As a high school student, Marsh earned spending money working at the Rex and remembers the experiences with fondness and nostalgia.

The entertainment center for years in Tower, the Rex operated every night except Monday. Inevitably, Marsh and his cronies found a use for it on Monday, too.

"We got one of those metal ice cream containers, the big cans, from the drugstore, and filled it with water. I had a key to the theater, and we picked up a bunch of popcorn bags there and lugged everything back across the street and up to the top of the Tower Mercantile, a two-story building with a flat roof—ideal for what we had in mind.

"We filled a few bags with water and waited until some unsuspecting soul passed by below, then we'd drop a bag over the edge. Even a near miss would soak the victim. One night we got a direct hit on the chief of police. The three of us went off that roof in about three jumps, down through Tony Gornick's yard, across the ball field and up into the woods. He never caught us."

Television also sounded the death knell for another Tower tradition: neighborhood skating rinks. Television's tiny, snowy, black and white pictures that broke ground for a new era in home entertainment in the 1950s lured many a family from outdoor activities into the living room.

"I'm almost sorry such a thing as television came into being," Marsh says, making an unexpected observation from a man who would share four decades of his life with microphones and TV cameras. But television cut into sandlot hockey and thinned out the skating crowds in Tower.

"It was the end of our rinks," Marsh says with an almost

imperceptible shake of his head. "Before television, they were the centers of everything."

In the biting cold winters that routinely sent temperatures well below zero, snow crunched and squeaked under boots as families with youngsters of all ages trudged to the rinks each night.

"Down at the baseball field we had one skating rink and one full-size hockey rink. The skating rink was full of older folks and little kids, and there were always at least 30 guys on the hockey rink. Fifteen below zero—it didn't make any difference. We organized our own games, and some nights you'd hardly get a chance to touch the puck. But we learned the basics: stick handling, passing, shooting and, above all, skating. Some of us younger guys would try to get there early so the older ones would let us play. They'd pick the younger guys to be goalies and, since I had the only real goalie stick in town, that's where I'd usually end up. But I learned quickly that it was more fun to be out on the ice shooting than in the goal being shot at.

"It was strictly snowbank hockey—was no such thing as high-sticking, cross-checking or other various and sundry crimes. If a guy tripped somebody, the others would take his stick and throw it out into a snowbank. The time it took him to go get it constituted the penalty."

In the post-Depression years, equipment was makeshift: cast-off hockey sticks carefully wrapped with black friction tape, an old chipped puck with the owner's initials deeply carved into both sides, no protective gear unless it was wooden slats sewn side by side into sugar sacks for shin pads.

"We bought our skates four or five sizes too big so they'd last a few years," Marsh recalls, "and fill 'em up with extra pairs of socks. Each year, as our feet grew, we'd wear one less layer of socks. With new skates, I'd have four or five pairs of socks on and, by the time the skates wore out, I'd be down to one pair.

"I took that custom to college with me when I played for Macalester. Doc Romnes, the hockey coach at the University of

Minnesota, would referee some of our games, and it was probably coincidental but it seemed that every time Doc refereed a Mac game, it was a good game for me. He talked to me several times about transferring to Minnesota. One of those times, he looked down at my feet and asked, 'What size are those skates?' I told him, and he nearly died. He said skates should be one and a half sizes smaller than street shoes. Mine were about three sizes larger."

Charlie Nelson's abiding love of sports and the outdoors was the biggest single influence in his son's development and sense of values.

"I wouldn't consider Dad a great philosopher, but the most important thing he taught me was, 'If you're going to do something, anything, do it as well as you can, your very best. Otherwise, you're wasting your time.' I've always tried to live by that code, even in the most trivial things."

Hunting and fishing were among the most important things in Charlie's life, and he passed that love on to Marsh.

"He played the way he worked: full time and making every minute count. The morning of a hunting or fishing trip he never had to shake me. I'd be out of bed on time, no matter how early it was."

A favorite duck hunting spot was Lost Lake south of Tower, but in those days only a few determined souls could get there over a forest trail that was muddy, wet and mostly invisible.

"You either had to have a boat that somebody dragged in and left, or you carried a canoe," Marsh remembers. "We'd leave the car on the road and still have three-quarters of a mile to go on foot over pretty rough, wet country. I was eight or nine, so I was limited to carrying the guns, a few decoys and our lunch. But Dad would throw a heavy sack of decoys over his shoulder then go for the canoe. It was on top of the car, a 1939 Chevy, and he'd just slide it off the roof and onto his back and away he'd go. This was no flimsy aluminum canoe, either. This was an 18-foot Old

Towne, a heavy devil with ribs and canvas and umpteen coats of paint. It was dark, and the trail was only a path through the woods. I'd go on ahead holding a flashlight, like a theater usher.

"And he could really handle that canoe. With Dad I never was scared, even in the roughest waves. On Everett Bay if you got a northerly blow the rollers would really kick up coming in off Big Bay, but the Old Towne was seaworthy and Dad was a master. He always taught me safety: in getting in or out, you walk down the center on the keel, never on the ribs. If you stepped to either side, you'd go over in a hurry."

Charlie Nelson died in 1972. Marsh's warm memories flood back as he talks.

"Duck hunting with Dad was a highlight. He bought me a little 20-gauge single shot and, strangely, I had a higher percentage of kills with that little shotgun than I ever did later with a 12-gauge automatic. Of course, there were more ducks then.

"I loved duck hunting: setting decoys and paddling back to shore, pulling the boat in, loading the guns, settling down in the blind to wait for something to happen. Sometimes, a pre-dawn flight would go over and it'd be too early to shoot, but there was the thrill of hearing them, listening to their wings and their squawking. It was great just being out there, even if all I did is shoot holes in the sky and come home empty-handed."

Then there was the day Charlie Nelson quit hunting forever.

"I'll never forget it," Marsh says with a rare frown. "He'd been out all day deer hunting, and he came home mad. He'd met another hunter coming out of the woods, they exchanged greetings and the stranger bragged about taking three sound shots— couldn't even see what he was shooting at. Dad was really upset. 'With nuts like that in the woods,' he said, 'I don't want to hunt anymore.' He cleaned his rifle, set it in a corner and never picked it up again."

Marsh's affection for his father shines through whenever he talks about his childhood.

"Dad had a variety of jobs while I was growing up. He was a sort of self-taught civil engineer: foreman on a dam project in southeastern Minnesota, down around Winona, and later supervisor of construction on a stretch of highway between Tower and Virginia. He also served as Tower's police chief for a few years, then he got on as a diamond driller in the Soudan mine. He worked underground until he retired in the mid 1950s. Not bad for a guy with only a third grade education.

"Dad and I were real close. He taught me much more than just safety in handling guns and canoes. He knew how to make the most of the good things that were available. He believed strongly that there's no free lunch—you get out of life what you put into it. Dad always had a handle on what was right and what was wrong, and he didn't use a Bible or law books to practice those things. He lived a better life, a cleaner life, a more honest life, than a lot of people. He wasn't much of a church-goer himself, but he lived his life close to nature and was always kind."

# CHAPTER THREE

# A Clash of Cymbals

S mall towns along Minnesota's Iron Ranges thrive on high school athletics. Every game is a major event—coffee-break conversation for days afterward.

Boys and girls long for the distinction of earning and wearing a varsity letter on a sweater or jacket. In his high school years, which ended in 1947, Marsh earned six of the coveted purple-and-gold "T-S" emblems, three each in basketball and football, the only two sports Tower-Soudan offered.

"I'd go to any lengths to get to the games when I was younger," he says, paging through a yellowing copy of the high school newspaper, the *TA-SA-HA*. ("We never had a yearbook in those days.")

"I finally hit on a sure way to see most of the games free and get to the district tournament: take music lessons. Now understand, I'm not—and wasn't then—the greatest musician who ever drew breath, so I picked the snare drum. They started me on the triangle.

"I finally got into the band, and the band played at every game.

By that time, I'd moved up to the cymbals. My big moment came on my first time out, when we were playing the *Star Spangled Banner* at the start of a basketball game: the big cymbal crash near the end. When you have only one note to play, you better get it right. My part had 63 bars of rest. I gave it 62. I smacked those cymbals together, and it was beautiful. It was also about two-and-a-half seconds too soon. The director, Reinhold Darm, threw his baton at me.

"The Tower-Soudan band in those days was excellent. After Darm left, a young, vibrant Charles Minelli, just out of the University of Minnesota, took over its direction. Darm's musical basics, plus Minelli's showmanship, came together to make the T-S band the talk of the Range in the 1940s. In fact, when the District 27 basketball tournament rolled around, the Virginia paper, the *Mesabi Daily News*, wrote: 'It's hard to predict the best team, but we all know Tower-Soudan has the best band.'"

Tower youngsters in those days, until they reached high school, had no organized sports.

"We played just for the fun of it," Marsh says with conviction, "not because our parents pushed us or drove us into it. But there wasn't much organization until Dean Carlson, our Presbyterian minister, put together a sort of junior softball league. Dean was the nearest we younger kids came to having a coach. He'd pile 10 or 12 of us into his 1940 Plymouth and take us to Gilbert, Mountain Iron or Virginia, or to the Indian school to play. Dean was mentor to many kids. He believed in youngsters and taught us all some important lessons—in life and in sports.

"The skating rinks in Tower-Soudan were filled every night, all winter long," Marsh recalls with a smile. "If there was a snowstorm and people couldn't skate they'd stay inside and go stir crazy until the caretaker could get down there with a team of horses to clear the ice.

"Joe Stack, the warming shack attendant, really controlled things. He smoked an old caked-up pipe constantly, and I can still see him, when the shack windows frosted over, holding that pipe to the glass to thaw out a peephole so he could watch the kids on the ice."

Soudan's rink had regulation-size dasher boards, like those in most arenas today, but the Tower hockey rink had sideboards only a foot high. "We spent a lot of time chasing pucks in snowbanks," Marsh recalls.

"I'm sure I was more proficient in hockey and baseball, two sports the school didn't have. One day, we got a bunch of guys together and went over to play Eveleth's high school team, which had just won another state championship. The Golden Bears beat us, but only by one goal. We thought, 'We're wasting our time playing basketball in school. We should have hockey in Tower.'

"On the other hand, if we'd had high school hockey, we might not have been able to field a basketball team. The school gym wasn't available for basketball practice except in season, and then only to the team, so except for backyard basketball hoops, there wasn't much opportunity for practice. On the other hand, the rinks were always there, so every kid grew up skating."

The janitors—Marsh's uncle, Elmer Gustafson, Alfred Bystrom or Johnny Helstrom—would sometimes open the school on weekends so the street jocks could shoot baskets on a real court. "Otherwise," Marsh says, "the place was locked up and nobody could use it except during school hours and for gym classes. Eventually, they got around to opening the school for five or six hours on Saturdays, but we could only get in if we had adult supervision."

His fondness for hockey started early and grew into a lifelong love. On the sly, he joined Soudan's city hockey team, the V-8s, while still a junior in high school. The team's main competition came from similar clubs in Ely, Mountain Iron, Gilbert and Virginia.

"If the coach found out I was playing for the city hockey team," he says, "I'd be off the basketball team. We played our home games in Soudan, so our school cheerleaders would watch the entrances to the rink and if our basketball coach, Mike Weinzierl, showed up at a game, they'd tip me off and I wouldn't play."

The V-8s were a lean team: only two forward lines and three defensemen, "Four, sometimes, if we were lucky," Marsh says. "We beat Virginia in the first round of a tournament one time and had to play Eveleth. We weren't in a class with Eveleth, but they had to go into overtime to beat us, 3-2. Our goalie, Leonard Roy, had 65 saves in that game and Eveleth's goalie had only eight—and they went to the national tournament in Toledo."

The team stumbled onto Leonard Roy by accident.

"Don Avikainen's brother was our regular goalie," Marsh recalls, reaching for an old photo of the team. "We were supposed to play International Falls one night, and he was to meet us there. When we got to the rendezvous point, there was no Avikainen. He had a job on the Range somewhere, and we stopped at a gas station to call around to find him. No luck. Finally, the station attendant said, 'You guys lookin' for a goalie? Tell you what. I got a friend who was a goalie for the Memorial Cup team at Fort Frances when he was 17 years old. He didn't like that bunch so he quit. He loves hockey, though, and I bet if you guys asked him, he'd play for you.'

"We finally found him. His name was Leonard Roy. He said, 'I ain't played for awhile but, sure, I'll be done with work in half an hour.'

"Well, we played at night, outside, in 30-below weather. Lucky there was no wind. The rink was next to the Falls bandshell, and there was a warming house so at least we didn't have to sit on a cold bench or stand in a snowbank between line changes. We could be inside.

"With Leonard Roy in the net we beat the Falls, hands down."

In the summers, nearly every alley or backyard had its homemade basketball court. Marsh's basket was over the garage doors. "In the winter, we'd have to shovel a wide path to the garage to shoot baskets. I sometimes wonder if that's why Dad let me put it there."

He warmly remembers the diligence of one Soudan youth, Don Avikainen, now of Silver Bay.

"Avi was a good example of what a kid can do if he truly wants to make something of himself. He could really find that hoop. He was in the alley back of his house every night, under the street light, even in a blizzard or 15 below, with those buckskin choppers on, shooting baskets all alone. He'd practice with a 14-inch rim, and a regulation basketball would hardly go through, but he'd never miss. He was one of our all-time stars in high school—the best shot I've ever seen, at any level."

The annual spring thaw added another dimension to backyard basketball: mud. Games were sloppy and players mud-splattered, so Charlie Nelson built a portable basket that could be moved into the comparatively dry street. "It was one of a kind," Marsh recalls. "The backboard was on two poles set on two upright braces so we could move it any place in the neighborhood.

"We never had any real coaching 'til high school. We could shoot pretty good, but we were weak in fundamentals: passing, dribbling, covering, things you have to learn.

"We put our own ball field together wherever we could find a dry, flat piece of ground. We played sandlot baseball, alley basketball and boot hockey. Nobody led us, but I think we had more fun doing it than kids growing up today. There's too much pressure on the little kids today—from parents and coaches—too much emphasis on winning. They've taken a lot of the fun out of it."

Basketball and football were the two school-sponsored sports, and Marsh played both with enthusiasm.

"One advantage in living in a small town is that if you want to make the team, there isn't much competition," Marsh says. "Our

23

senior class had only 13 boys, and 12 were on the football team. The 13th—and the biggest guy in school—was John Zobitz. Unfortunately, after his dad died John had to go home after school and run the family's grocery store."

Basketball was king among high school sports in the 1940s, and the state tournament was Minnesota's No. 1 high school sporting event. Marsh had a taste of the glory.

"It was 1946, and we went to the state. I was just grateful to go. I wasn't a regular, but I did play either forward or guard on the second five.

"They called us the 'Giants of the North' because our center, Stenfeldt 'Hank' Peterson, was six-foot-four, and Frank Stepan and Don Avikainen were six-foot-two. We lost the first game to Mountain Lake but came back to win the consolation title, beating Roseau and Minneapolis Washburn."

Marsh's senior year in basketball was marked by triumphs and disappointments.

"We struggled through the first round of the district tournament to beat Virginia and then met Ely in the semi-finals. We handled Ely with ease in the last game of the regular season, but in the District 27 tourney they beat us in a close game and went on to lose the Region 7 final in overtime to Denfeld, the eventual state champions. Boy, we'd have loved a whack at those Hunters. When you're a senior on a losing team in the tournaments, you're losing your last game in school."

American Legion baseball came to Tower after Marsh's junior year in high school with football-basketball coach Weinzierl in charge. Weinzierl promptly picked Marsh as captain and told him to run the team.

"It was the first time I'd ever played on a team. We had only hand-me-down uniform shirts from the Tower city team—no baseball pants. They did give us new caps," Marsh says.

A former high school basketball rival, George Marsnik, urged him to try out for the Ely city team, the BluSox, after graduation.

"I got on as second baseman. As a matter of fact, the guy I followed was Jim Klobuchar, now a columnist for the Minneapolis *Star Tribune*. My good friend, the late Ole Haugsrud [an original owner of the Minnesota Vikings], was happy about that. Ole said, more than once, 'Next time Klobuchar says something bad in his column about the Vikings, I'll remind him that Marsh Nelson beat him out for second base in his hometown of Ely.'"

Klobuchar remembers it differently. "Marsh and I never competed," he says. "I played two seasons for the team and worked the next summer in Duluth—which Nelson probably should have done himself. Anyhow, we never played on the same field and I can't say I was ever placed on anybody's waiver list!"

The BluSox played in the Arrowhead League. "We had good athletes," Marsh says, "serious about winning: the Marsniks, the Ellioffs, Manager Fred Banks, Donnie Kuzma, Dick Buckley, the Landa twins—Joe and Stan—and tremendous support from the fans. It was right after the war, there was a lot of money around and people craved entertainment. It wasn't uncommon to have a couple thousand people turn out on a Sunday afternoon for a home game. I think the support Ely later generated for the national Legion tournament, and a number of state tournaments they've hosted since, is an outgrowth of the old BluSox of the 1940s and early 1950s."

Marsh played for the BluSox three years, until the summer of 1951, when Tower entered the fledgling Mesabi League with a new team, the Colts. "I figured I'd better go with the home team," he says. He joined the Tower Colts as a pitcher. "The late Sulo Lundgren was the big pitcher for Mountain Iron, and he and I had some great pitching duels.

"William 'Doc' Heim of Cook was president of the Mesabi League, and Ken Saari in Mountain Iron was the guy who made it go. Kenny was a remarkable guy. He operated from a wheelchair, keeping statistics, keeping track of schedules, umpires, players. He and Doc ran a good league."

Charlie Nelson was his son's most vocal fan. "He never missed a home game when I was playing," Marsh remembers.

Some other fans recall Charlie Nelson's pride in his son and his enthusiasm for the game a little differently.

"You could hear him for a block," says Ray Peil with a chuckle. "According to Charlie, Marsh was never wrong. If there were mistakes or errors, Marsh never made them."

A teammate, Herb Lamppa [later a Tower mayor and a St. Louis County commissioner] remembers a time when Charlie Nelson's sideline coaching was too much even for Marsh.

"Marsh was a great competitor," Herb recalls. "He put his heart and soul into any game he was playing. He was a sparkplug with a lot of innovative ideas. He was a good sport, but a hard loser and never went into a game with any thoughts of losing.

"One game, Charlie was sitting in the crowd on the edge of the ball field, yelling encouragement as usual. Marsh was pitching; I was catching. You could hear Charlie's voice above everybody else, and he was making some rather pointed remarks about the umpire's family of origin.

"You could see that Marsh was irritated. He took it for a couple of innings. Finally, he took off his cap, slammed it to the ground, stomped on it, walked over to the terrace and pointed his finger at his dad. I don't know what he said, but when he finished he walked back to the mound, picked up his cap and went on with the game. Charlie was a lot quieter, at least for that game."

Marsh played with abandon and flair. Bruce Bennett wrote about Marsh's "sensational diving catches" in a *Duluth News-Tribune* column not long ago. That column sparked a memory for Marsh:

"We were playing Eddie Feigner's 'King and His Court' [a four- man traveling exhibition softball team]. One guy hit a drive up the middle, and I dove through the air and speared it. The next time the guy came around to second base he called time, walked over to me, grabbed my glove and said, 'So that's the damn thing that robbed me of a hit!' He threw it down and jumped on it."

Don Avikainen recalls an occasion less stellar. "Marsh was contending for the Mesabi League batting title in one of the final games of the season against Cook. Marsh laughed when he heard that a minister would be pitching. He laughed harder when the guy came out to the mound in a softball uniform. Marsh turned to me and said, 'Here's where I fatten up my batting average with this guy.' No way. He struck out three times."

Then there was the game in Biwabik that was played with a strange umpire. "Nobody knew him," said Avi. "He musta been an old softball umpire because he called balls and strikes from behind the mound. He was a ponderous man in a wide-brimmed straw hat and bib overalls. He and Marsh had a big rhubarb on the mound about something. Marsh had his finger on the guy's chest and I heard him say, 'You can't throw me out unless I use abusive language'—something Marsh never did. The guy threw him out anyway."

It wasn't the first or last time Marsh Nelson was thrown out of a ballgame.

"We were playing on the Nett Lake Indian reservation one day and the sheriff, Ira White, an Indian himself, was the umpire. He was a fine man, Ira was, but not what you'd call an impartial umpire. I can't remember the infraction—real or imagined—but he not only threw me out of the game, he ordered me off the reservation."

Earlier, in another game, modern technology cost the Ely team a base runner.

"Must have been the summer of '49," Marsh says with a grin. "Jets were just coming into their own, and there were a few at the Duluth air base. I forget who we were playing, but one of our guys got a base hit and was starting to lead off first, a few steps off the bag, when a jet roared over, low. Everybody in the ball park looked up, including the players and the umpires—everybody, that is, except the opposing pitcher and first baseman. The pitcher calmly threw the ball over to first and the base umpire had to stop looking at the jet to call 'You're out!' The pitcher and first basemen must have been the only ones who'd seen a jet before."

Marsh adjusts easily to situations and rarely worries about events and conditions he can't control. It's a trait he learned early and one that has served him well throughout life.

"I just figure there's no point fretting about something you can't do anything about," he says with a shrug. "For instance, I never had a job I didn't like, so I don't worry about going to work every day. You just have to concentrate on the good things, and there's something good about every job. I even liked my job at the box factory. We got paid by the hour, and it wasn't much, but everybody there had pride in his work."

The Lennartson box factory on Lake Vermilion's Pike Bay was his first real job after high school.

"There were two sawmills in town that supplied the factory. We had contracts all over the Midwest, judging from the names of places we stamped on the boxes and crates.

"Talk about working by the bell! The buzzer sounded at 8 in the morning, and you went to work. It went off again at noon and again at 12:30 when lunch was over. You'd work 'til 4:30 and 'boom!' the buzzer would sound and everything stopped—immediately—even the nailing machines, right in the middle of the process, no matter what position the nails were in."

Marsh started as a laborer and quickly moved up to making crates. His description of the nailing machine is animated by waving arms and wriggling fingers. "It's hard to describe, but you put the pieces of wood on a kind of frame, then pushed it into a slot-like affair. When everything was in place, the operator would step on his foot lever and all the nails would be driven into place at once.

"It was probably the second-best place in town to work, after the Soudan mine, which paid a lot more. The thing I liked about it was, you went to work with the buzzer at 8 in the morning, and you quit with the buzzer at 4:30. You worked your eight hours and you were done. You never took your work home with you. At 4:30, you scooted out, got on your bike or into your car or walked home. You could go fishing or do whatever you wanted to do."

But the box factory was only a job. It was the curve in Highway 35 south of Tower that changed Marsh Nelson's life.

# CHAPTER FOUR

# Mac Days

T hat's the spot, just ahead," Marsh says, pointing. On this crisp October Saturday he's driving to Tower for a day of partridge hunting.

"About a year out of high school I started working for the state highway department—engineering aide for a survey crew. I liked the work and the people I worked with. I never intended to go to college; wasn't thinking much beyond playing baseball and working for the highway department. But I was getting steady encouragement from our project engineer, John Harrison, who thought I could be a civil engineer. I appreciated his interest, but didn't take it too seriously."

He slows the car to a near crawl.

"One day, we were working here, between Tower and Aurora. My boss, Einar Koivisto, said they'd arranged it so my time in college would count toward service with the state, as long as I was studying engineering and working summers with the department. Suddenly, then and there, it just hit me. I made the decision to go on to school."

The decision was a milestone.

"I think everything good that's happened in my life since then started right here, on this curve, with that decision. Every time I drive by this spot I think about that."

The decision took form in September of 1950.

"I considered the University of Minnesota," he said, "but it was right after the war, and the main campus in Minneapolis was overloaded with vets. There were 40,000 students there in 1950. I wanted a smaller school."

Marsh picked Macalester College in St. Paul, a Presbyterian school, partly because of its excellent academic standing, but mainly for its hockey program—and Tommy Noyes.

"Tommy was the son of our long-time Tower school superintendent, William Noyes. He was captain of the Macalester hockey team, and when he'd come home on breaks he'd play in our little pickup hockey games. I thought to myself, 'Man, if he made team captain, I think there's a chance for me. Maybe I can be captain of that team someday, too.'"

Tom Noyes remembers Marsh, too, but in an earlier game. "Marsh was an intense hockey player, even as a youngster," he says. "One day I was at the hockey rink at the football field in Tower watching a pickup game in which Marsh was involved. I'd guess he was about 10 or 12 years old. Suddenly, Marsh yelled 'Time out!' and rushed to a snowbank to relieve himself. He came back to the rink and yelled 'Time in!' and the game went on. I should explain that there were no toilet facilities, and it wasn't uncommon to see snow piles utilized in that fashion. The difference was that Marsh wasn't about to miss any of the game for nature's call. I've told this story many times when people comment on Marsh's success to illustrate the drive he has."

Marsh dutifully enrolled in pre-engineering at Macalester but, about midway through the sophomore year, he began to realize he wasn't cut out to be an engineer.

"For one thing, if I'd continued in engineering I'd have had to transfer to the university, something I didn't want to do. Besides, calculus wasn't my cup of tea. I considered coaching and teaching as a career, and plodded along for about a year. Then I read something Herb Drew, late coach at Cloquet, said. Herb had just lost a tough one and, when a newsman asked him how he felt, he said, 'There must be an easier way to make a living!' Coming from him, that gave me something to think about, and I changed my major again. First, the end of my highway career; now the end of my teaching, too."

Despite Tower's distance from St. Paul, sports, friendships, and hunting and fishing trips with his dad still drew Marsh back to Tower at every opportunity. Hitchhiking was easy but risky.

"There was nothing like today's I-35 super highway, just old Highway 61, which was an antique even then. One day I was standing on North Snelling Avenue with my thumb out and a big 'Ely' sign taped on my suitcase—Ely was more familiar to most drivers than Tower, and it had fewer letters. A shiny black car stopped and picked me up. The two guys inside were advance men for one of Billy Graham's films, *Oiltown, U.S.A.* They must have thought they had divine protection. That ride was a real white-knuckler. They passed on curves and blind hills on that old single-lane highway, at speeds that set your teeth on edge. Their faith must have been unshakable.

"I've always had more than average faith in the Lord, but I got to thinking, 'This is ridiculous! We may be testing the Lord a bit too much.' When we got to where Highway 23 cuts off for Duluth, I told them to drop me off. If they drove like that on 61, I sure didn't want to be with them on 23 with its curves, hills and dales!"

Marsh immersed himself in Macalester's social and athletic life. He earned four letters each in varsity baseball and hockey and, in his senior year, was president of the Lettermen's Club as well as secretary for another campus organization, the Athenian Society.

With the help of the athletic department, he had several good jobs during his Macalester days. Unquestionably, the best was one any red-blooded American college male would have killed to get: Marsh Nelson was live-in janitor in the women's dormitory. "I got the job when the guy who had it, basketball star Bob McDonald—later the legendary coach in Chisholm—transferred to the university in Duluth.

"Jim Grothe and I shared a room in the basement of Wallace Hall, the women's residence. One of our duties was to lock every door at night, except the main entrance, and unlock them in the morning. This, of course, was to discourage the women from coming and going all hours of the night—as well as preventing boyfriends from doing the same. There we were, locked in with 250 single women!

"Our room was flanked by the laundry on one side and the rec room on the other. We had to keep our room door locked because there was always plenty of female traffic going past. It was pure hell," he says with a grin.

It was, by all accounts, the best job on campus. Room and board was free, and there was a key to the kitchen so ice cream and midnight snacks were easy. But the job did have rocky moments.

"Once in awhile, we'd be roused up at one or two in the morning when some young lady put something she shouldn't into the latrine and plugged it up. We'd get out the plunger and other gear and try to unplug the biffy. Of course, all the women on that floor would turn out to watch, laugh and offer encouragement."

As a resident, Marsh had the inside track when it came time to crown "King Wally" for Wallace and Bigelow Halls, an annual accolade bestowed on a popular senior male student.

"I won because they all knew me. I worked there."

Among Marsh's friends was Ed "Boodie" Borkon, now a Twin Cities attorney, whose talent for voice impressions of celebrities was uncanny.

"He could imitate Gary Cooper, Walter Brennan, Peter Lorre and a host of other stars of the day to a 'T'," Marsh recalls. "He could also do a perfect Charles J. Turck." One cold spring night, Borkon's impersonation of Turck, the Macalester president, was put to use, at Marsh's urging.

"They'd turned down the heat in the dorms a little early that year, and it was chilly, so we talked Boo into calling the heating plant super."

Borkon got on the phone and, in a deep, pompous voice, said, "This is Doctor Turck speaking. The boys are complaining that the rooms are cold. Please turn the heat back on." The radiators were clanging within minutes.

Instead of winning kudos, Borkon himself became the target of another prank by his fellow conspirators. Another Marsh Nelson crony, "Duke" Herman, had a girlfriend who worked in the office of Dean Wilhelmus Bryant. She pirated a sheet of official stationery on which Marsh and his friends typed a note to Borkon, ordering him, in no uncertain terms, to report to the dean's office at his earliest opportunity. "Ed really worried that somebody had found out about the phone call to the heating plant. We let him sweat for a few days until he was sure he'd be suspended, then we let him off the hook."

Marsh's Wallace Hall roommate, Jim Grothe, struggled with two constant challenges: keeping his studies up and his weight down.

"Jim was state wrestling champion and played football at Mac," Marsh says. "He practiced his wrestling holds on me, and I'd make sure he studied. He wrestled as a light heavyweight, but should have been a heavyweight because he sure had a problem staying under 175. Many times, on the morning of a match he'd be three or four pounds overweight. He wouldn't eat all day, not even a pear. Since we didn't have a sauna at Mac, Jim would go over to the shower room, turn on three or four showers at once, as hot as he could stand, and sit there for a couple of hours cooking off extra fat."

Marsh remembers hitting only one home run in college baseball.

"It was in a game that almost wasn't played," he says with a grin. "We were to meet St. Olaf one Saturday afternoon, but apparently nobody was sure where. We thought the game was scheduled for Northfield. St. Olaf thought it was at Macalester. The buses must have passed on the way because we showed up at St. Olaf and they ended up in St. Paul. Our coach got on the phone with their coach and they came to an agreement. The Oles came home and we played there. There was a terrace around the field but no fence. I hit a ball between center and right field and it must have rolled 500 feet down the hill. It sure wasn't a fly. As I recall, we won."

His less glamorous extracurricular assignments included manicuring the baseball diamond, putting lines on the football field before games, handing out towels and equipment to the football team and caring for Macalester's outdoor hockey rink.

"I don't know why, but we got better ice when we flooded after midnight. Less wind, maybe. If you want good ice, though, you have to use warm water. We had a homemade affair the shops rigged up, just a plain barrel with runners. A tap on the bottom fed water into a pipe that had a bunch of holes in it. We'd attach a burlap gunny sack around the pipe, and the hot water would drip into the burlap. As we pushed the contraption across the ice, we'd cover about five or six feet with a single swing. It was a Rube Goldberg version of the modern Zamboni."

The rink faced busy Snelling Avenue, which sometimes presented a problem for the Scots' goalie, Dwight Atherton.

"Dwight was fascinated by the noise of those 'square-wheeled' streetcars that rumbled past about every 15 minutes," Marsh recalls. "He'd look out at a streetcar and our coach, Hank Frantzen, would yell: 'Dwight, you cockroach! Forget about the streetcars on Snelling. Watch the puck on this rink and we'll all be better off!'

"Hank referred to everybody as cockroach—he pronounced it 'cock-er-roach'—a term of endearment, if he liked you. He had a job with a St. Paul insurance company, so he'd call me every day to ask how the ice was. If I told him it was good, he'd call practice and I'd tack a notice on the bulletin board: 'All cockroaches will report for hockey practice at four o'clock.' They knew who they were."

Marsh Nelson's years as star center for Macalester are still remembered by alumni more than 35 years later. Although he captained the Scots in his junior and senior years, his natural modesty downplays an impressive record.

"One season, we played Gustavus Adolphus in Mankato. It was awful! The Gusties weren't a strong team that year, and we beat them 16-1. The scorekeeper must have been a friend of mine because I had five goals and eight assists. I guess he'd give me an assist if I was just on the ice."

Charlie Nelson saw his son play only one college hockey game.

"It was in the old Duluth Curling Club against UMD, and I hate to say it but we got robbed by the officials, and the Bulldogs beat us 5-3. Hank Jensen—later my very dear friend—was referee. I still respect him as much as anybody I've ever met, not only for his knowledge of the game, but also for the kind of man he is.

"We got all the bad calls. When the game was over, Hank Frantzen went over to him, stuck his nose into Jensen's face and said, 'Jensen, you cockroach! You got eyes like a dead fish!'"

In 1952, during his sophomore year, Macalester handed Marsh Nelson a solid gold opportunity that set a course for the rest of his life.

"They were starting a campus radio station, and the *Mac Weekly* carried a notice for auditions. I'd never done anything like that before, but I'd sure listened to a lot of radio. I didn't expect much, but I went over anyway. I was stunned when I got the job as sports announcer. I started with five minutes of sports two or three times a week." Later, when the station decided to carry Macalester basketball, Marsh did the play-by-play. He had found a life's work.

Most of his learning came through on the job training, but he received professional guidance from an unexpected source when WLOL's Dick Enroth, then the Twin Cities' top sportscaster and the "Voice of the Minneapolis Lakers," went to Macalester for a Career Day.

"Kids who wanted to be engineers met with an engineer, those who wanted to get into retail sales would talk with a salesman, and so forth. I was interested in radio and TV so I went to see Enroth."

When Marsh walked in, Enroth was sitting alone, feet crossed on top of the instructor's desk, hands folded across his chest.

"We had a lot of time to talk, and I got to know him a little," Marsh remembers.

"How long could you talk about that chair over there, without any preparation?" Enroth asked.

"About 30 seconds," Marsh replied.

Enroth shook his head. "With some experience, you should be able to ad lib about that chair for at least 30 minutes." He then proceeded to give Marsh a lesson in filling empty air time.

"There's steel in that chair, and part of it's wood. You can go back and trace the development of a piece of steel, back to the mines up north. The coal for it is probably mined in Pennsylvania. The wood is processed in Grand Rapids. You can talk about crafting it, finishing it. You should be able to get at least a half-hour's chatter out of that chair."

Marsh and Enroth struck up a friendship, and the veteran

broadcaster invited the neophyte to the WLOL studios on several occasions.

"Dick was a major influence on me," Marsh says. "He was a great talent. In those days, when the Lakers were playing out of town, he'd do radio re-creations of the games. It was almost unbelievable how he'd create the atmosphere of being right there on the scene. He was always a little behind the actual play because the statistics came over on ticker tape, the kind that the stock market uses—the glass dome that spits out a narrow stream of paper. Those reports were just like line scores in baseball, no details. Dick's imagination supplied the details and color, and he'd use recorded crowd noise as background."

Enroth made it sound easy: "When you've seen every Laker home game for years, you know where Pollard shoots from," he told Marsh. "You imagine him dancing down the floor, into the front court. You know Doogy Martin's style, and everybody knows George Mikan's favorite shot is from just to the left side of the lane. It's just a matter of knowing the game and the players."

Marsh's admiration is apparent. "Sometimes, I swear, he sounded more enthusiastic doing re-creations than when he was calling live games. "

Enroth's guidance was invaluable, but Marsh got a needed ego boost in the form of an unsolicited remark from a female fan. Marsh was calling Macalester basketball on a regular basis by that time and, one day on campus, he was approached by a mature, stylish woman.

"Young man, you make those broadcasts so exciting, I'd rather stay home and listen than go to the games."

"Afterward, a friend of mine asked if I knew who that was. I didn't, of course. He said it was Mrs. Turck, the wife of the president of Macalester College. That very kind remark started me thinking about making broadcasting a career."

Macalester graduated Marsh Nelson with a bachelor's degree

in economics and political science in June 1954. "It was about as far removed from what I was to do with my life as you can get," he says, settling back with a glass of iced tea on the redwood deck of his home in Duluth's Lakeside area. But the broadcast career that would follow would have to wait a few years.

# CHAPTER FIVE

# A Jock in Olive Drab

In the early 1950's North Korea invaded its southern neighbor, and selective service was in full swing. College draft deferments lasted only as long as the student was in school and doing acceptable work. After graduation, the male student was expected to fulfill his military obligation. The Ely draft board told Marsh he wouldn't be called until late fall of 1956. He decided not to wait.

"I figured nobody'd hire me knowing I'd be drafted soon, so I volunteered for the draft and went the first part of July. By that time, I'd made up my mind about a career, and I figured I'd use the GI Bill for radio school when I got out."

Like hundreds of young men before him, Marsh reported in at the old Federal Building in Minneapolis to be sworn in as a private soldier in the United States Army. With a load of other inductees, he boarded a bus for Fort Leonard Wood in Missouri. It took the Army a week and a half to decide it didn't have room for the newcomers there, so it was back on the bus again for Camp

Chaffee, Arkansas. In that garden spot, Marsh and his fellow inductees survived eight weeks of basic training.

"Most college graduates at that time were being assigned to Nike anti-aircraft missiles, so I went to Fort Bliss, Texas, for training as a guided missile radar operator. In the spring of 1955 there was a lot of speculation as to where we'd go from there. New missile sites were opening up all over the country, including Chicago and the Twin Cities, and those of us from the Midwest hoped to get either place. They sent me to Virginia, to a hamlet named Fox Hill. It isn't even on a road map."

Battalion headquarters were at nearby Fort Monroe, Virginia, but Fox Hill, where Marsh's missile Battery A was located, was the boondocks: one general store, one drugstore, one gasoline station and five Methodist churches. The place also had a strong softball tradition. Some of the top athletes in the area played on the Fort Monroe teams. One of the players there was Bob Saunders, considered by many as among the three best softball pitchers in America. Saunders also played for the Fox Hill city team.

"Fox Hill's team took on the best teams who traveled the east coast between Florida and New England," Marsh says. "Many of those games would go 12 to 15 innings, until Fox Hill would score, because nobody—nobody—ever got a run off Saunders. In many of his innings, there were nine pitches and the side was out."

Later, when the Fort Monroe league formed an all-star team, Marsh was catching and Saunders pitching.

"Never in my life have I ever seen anyone throw a ball like he did. When I'd warm him up before a game, I had to wear a face mask and chest protector. We got to be friends when we played on the all-stars, but we still played for our own teams in the regular Army league. I came to bat one night when we were playing against each other. I'd played baseball in Tower and Ely—Legion ball and town league—and I'd played in college, but I'd never had that feeling before, facing a pitcher. I stood in the batter's box and thought to myself, 'What the hell am I doing here?'

"They were ahead about 10-0. When I came to the plate, he kinda winked at me and said, 'I've got a good pitch for you here.' To this day I don't understand how, but I just knew he was going to throw me a changeup. When it came, I socked it over the light poles. If he hadn't said something to me, and if I hadn't guessed that changeup was coming, I'd have stood there and listened to 'em go by. Those fast balls sounded good but you never saw 'em. You'd better be starting your swing while he was winding up. If a good hitter tried to time his fast ball, his riser or drop sent 'em back to the bench."

The Fort Monroe assignment was an extra bonus for Marsh: the continuation of a lifelong interest in the Civil War.

"Jefferson Davis was imprisoned there in the late 1860s, and I'd visit his old casemate cell often. You could stand in there alone and imagine the old man, sitting in solitary, not even allowed to talk to anyone. And right off from shore was Hampton Roads, the scene of that famous fight between the two ironclads, the Monitor and Merrimack. It was a great place to reflect on your heritage."

Of all the sports Marsh played in the Army, football was least memorable.

"During the fall of 1955, I played on the Fort Monroe football squad, kicking field goals and point-afters. When we played Fort Belvoir and Fort Eustace we were, to say the least, a little over our heads. In their backfield, Fort Eustace had an All-American quarterback named Eddie Price from Texas, and their halfbacks were Dick Gregory of Minnesota and Harlan Carl, who was just out of Wisconsin. Stan Wallace of the Chicago Bears was the fullback. I don't mind saying we didn't do too well against Fort Eustace. In one game, they buried us something like 60 to 10."

But Marsh Nelson playing hockey was Marsh Nelson in his element. Largely through the efforts of Macalester coach Hank

Frantzen and Hank's friendship with Minnesota's John Mariucci, Marsh was selected to try out for the 1956 Olympic hockey team coached by "Maroosh," a living legend.

"One of my great treasures is a copy of my orders from Department of Defense," Marsh says. "Along with another private named Bill Cleary, I was ordered to report to the Minneapolis airbase where Mariucci was putting the Olympic team together."

They spent two months with the Olympic hopefuls. Cleary, a former All-American at Harvard, made the team. After the final game, played in Des Moines, Marsh was one of the last players cut.

"I should have had at least a half-dozen goals that night. Cleary and Dick Rodenheiser kept setting me up—feeding me the puck—but, while I could skate with the best of 'em, my shot wouldn't break a pane of glass. Despite their best efforts, I scored only one."

Cleary went on to become head hockey coach of the Harvard Crimson.

Marsh returned to Fort Monroe just in time to join the basketball all-stars then forming. He made the squad that played in the Second Army tournament at Fort Knox, Kentucky.

"I learned where some of the taxpayers' money went. The Fort Knox Tankers played four games in four nights—in four different uniforms!"

It was a class act, that Fort Knox team.

"They could beat any college team in those days," Marsh says, "with guys like Furman's Frank Selvy, Frank Ramsey of the Boston Celtics, a kid by the name of Jim Jones who was All Big Ten from Ohio State. We didn't even get far enough to play 'em."

Typically, Marsh never let military duties interfere with athletics.

"I played everything I could, a sort of 'jock of all trades.' Our C.O., Captain Edmund Wells, insisted our battery be better than the other outfits. He asked me to go out for everything they had, in every competition that came down the pike. He'd call me in and say, 'Nelson, can you do this or that?' I did a little bit of everything: football, volleyball, softball, horseshoes, badminton. As a matter of fact, I didn't do much for the Army from September to the following March except play sports. It was a pretty good life. We could always get time off for sports. Much of what we did was waiting, anyway. Missile radar operators were on guard, 'watchful waiting' for an incoming attack. We'd be on duty six hours at the radar van and off 18. In those off hours, you could do anything you wanted to."

He spent one and a half months on the Olympic hockey team, two months with the Second Group football team as kicker, about three weeks on the basketball team and another week or two playing horseshoes. The horseshoes came shortly after he returned from Fort Knox.

"The captain told me about the Fort Monroe horseshoe tournament and asked me if I could play. I'd only played in Tower, out behind Martilla's drugstore, but I had my own style and practiced a lot. I'd learned the 'Bunker Hill' end-over-end slop toss and got pretty good at it. It was fairly easy to master but, because you tossed the shoe with the lugs up, it had to hit the ground just right or it'd slide on by. I'd learned from Stanley Hill—we called him 'Bunker'—back in Tower, the most ambidextrous athlete I've ever known. He could throw equally well with either hand.

"In the final match, I was up against a guy who'd been state champion in Ohio. We were both tossing about 75 percent ringers that day, but I edged him two out of three games."

Participation in novel sports didn't stop with horseshoes.

"I also teamed up with a friend from Virginia, Minnesota— Jim Johnson, who later taught school in Duluth—to play badminton. We won the Norfolk area doubles championship. It was a tough war."

The Army sent Specialist 3 Marsh Nelson home to Tower with an honorable discharge in June 1956. He hung around town that summer, driving a truck for the city for a couple of months, hunting and fishing, and finally enrolled in October at Brown Institute of Broadcasting in Minneapolis.

"I was looking around for a room in the Cities, and it was a kind of coincidence, I guess, because six of us got together and rented a house in the Midway district between Minneapolis and St. Paul. I'd been in the service with three of the guys, and the other two had been schoolmates at Macalester."

One of the friends was long-time Range acquaintance and former Army buddy, Jack Davies, later to become a state senator and appellate court judge. Davies, a journalism graduate of Minnesota's Murphy Hall, had a job as sports editor at KSTP, whose University Avenue broadcast studios four blocks away sits squarely between the Twin Cities. In fact, Stanley Eugene Hubbard, KSTP's venerable founder, had placed a vertical red line on the station's glass front doors and decreed it to be the dividing line between Minneapolis on the left and St. Paul on the right.

While attending sessions at Brown Institute, Marsh started haunting the KSTP newsroom with Jack Davies and was soon helping to write and edit television sports scripts, without pay, for the on-air personalities.

It was a new kind of journalism in the early television days, and everyone was learning to handle the medium.

"I worked with Jack for about a month at 'K-S' until he resigned to devote full time to law school," Marsh says. "The late Julian Hoshal, a great guy who taught a lot of us about the craft of television writing, was news director. When Jack left, he took me in to Julian and said, 'I've decided to quit but I've brought you my replacement and he's better than I am.' It was the biggest break I ever got in this business. It's not every day you get a chance like that at a station that pioneered local television news. If I hadn't started there, I don't know where I'd have ended up."

That news-weather-sports block at 10 p.m. on Channel 5 was one of the best in the nation, the talk of the entire Upper Midwest.

"The late Bill Ingram did the news, with that wink at the end. Johnny Morris was our weatherman. Dick Nesbitt was the No. 1 sports man on Twin Cities television at the time, and his assistant was Al Tighe, who took over after Dick's death. They were the first real anchor team in the Midwest and were all skilled professionals."

Dick Nesbitt's background was impressive. He knew what he was talking about because he'd been an athlete. Among other titles, he held the all-time punting record for Drake University and also had played professional football with the Chicago Bears. But the individualistic Nesbitt often confounded his listeners, as well as sports colleagues, by refusing to run with the pack on issues.

"He made up his own mind," Marsh says. "In those days, the sports corps was howling for Warmath's scalp [Murray Warmath, Minnesota head football coach who succeeded Bernie Bierman]. Murray had a couple of bad seasons and the Alumni Association, the press and the rest of the world were calling for his resignation or his head. Nes wouldn't join in. He'd say, 'I've known a lot of coaches, and I've played for a few. I'd rather be a booster than a knocker.'"

Writing for broadcast—where the words are spoken aloud— often presents challenges that print journalists can avoid or ignore, as Marsh learned one night.

"The Gophers' quarterback, Bobby Cox, was injured in practice just before a game with Michigan and couldn't make the trip to Ann Arbor. I was writing the story for Nesbitt's 10 p.m. sports. I asked him how he wanted to script it: 'Gophers travel to Ann Arbor without Cox,' or 'Gophers to play Michigan with Cox out?' He looked across the desk at me and said, 'Forget the whole thing!'"

Nesbitt and Marsh formed a close friendship that was based on mutual respect.

"Nes would say we got along because he couldn't read and I couldn't type. I took 'Typing for Athletes' at Macalester—hunt and peck. One night I was working on a story about the Pirates getting three runs in the seventh inning. I hit the 'N' instead of the 'R' key and it came out 'three nuns.' Nes usually read cold copy on the air but, this time, he caught it in time. Later, he said, 'You'll get me in trouble with my Catholic friends!'"

Nesbitt sometimes made his own mistakes.

"In those days, everything was live," Marsh says. "We didn't have videotape and damn little film. One night I gave him a story about a small southern Minnesota high school playing the Faribault School for the Deaf. He read it 'School for the Blind.' Five minutes after he got off the air, the coach called and said, 'Nesbitt, I know we aren't the best team in the state, but we're not so bad we have to play blind kids!'"

Not all of what Marsh learned from Nesbitt was necessarily good or comforting to television producers.

"He used to give directors fits," Marsh recalls, "because he'd arrive on set at the very last minute. Some nights, the Standard Oil theme was playing as he walked into the studio and I'd hand him his script. He'd settle into his chair, run his fingers through his thinning hair and, when the red tally lights on the camera blinked on, he'd wave and say, 'Hi, everybody! You're lookin' great tonight!'"

That same habit of last-minute frenzy would become a Marsh Nelson trademark.

# CHAPTER SIX

# Signing on at KDAL

Dick Nesbitt looked across his desk at Al Tighe and winked. "If you want to go over there, Al, I'm a friend of the owners. I'll put in a word for you."

The easy banter in the KSTP sports office concerned a staff vacancy that might result from the rumored departure of veteran sportscaster Frank Buetel from WTCN, a competing Twin Cities television station.

Tighe looked up from his typewriter, shook his head and smiled. "No thanks. Think I'll stick around K-S for awhile. But, it looks like there are several other sports openings. One's at KDAL, up in Duluth. Don Dahl is leaving."

At the mention of Duluth, Marsh Nelson's ears pricked up. "Gee, maybe I should take a shot at that one," he said.

In mock surprise, Tighe and Nesbitt looked over at Marsh standing at a clattering teletype machine.

"Sure, why not?" Nesbitt said. "The PD [program director] at KDAL is Earl Henton. Why don't you give him a call—on Stanley Hubbard's nickel!"

Marsh remembers the day well.

"A lot of breaks in this business depend on timing, being in the right place at the right time. It was one of those times. I picked up the phone, called Henton, and he told me to send up a tape. I had some pretty good ones in the sports file because, on a couple of occasions, Nes had said, 'You do the interview. People see enough of my ugly face.' These two were with Joe Louis and Detroit Tigers outfielder Al Kaline. I sent the tapes and waited.

"In a day or so, I got a call from the 'Earl of Henton' asking me to come to Duluth for an interview. When I drove up there the following weekend, he and General Manager Odin Ramsland were waiting, along with Rex Hudson, the radio sales manager, and Earl Jacott from TV sales. We talked awhile and Henton hired me on the spot.

"Talk about timing! If my audition tapes hadn't arrived just when they did, the station was all set to hire Bob Junkert [late sports director at WDSM-TV, now KBJR-TV] the next day!"

KDAL's radio and television studios in 1958 were on the second floor of the Bradley Building on the southeast corner of Lake Avenue and Superior Street in downtown Duluth. The radio station had been on the air since 1936 with call letters that reflected the initials of KDAL's founder, Dalton Alexander Le-Masurier. In 1954 KDAL-TV signed on as Duluth's third television station.

LeMasurier was a serious, disciplined visionary, a perfectionist who set high standards for his people and rewarded them generously when they met those standards. He constantly stimulated every employee to look for and try new ideas. He led daily "post mortem" sessions with his production staff, reviewing the previous day's telecasts—including such details as camera angles and microphone placement—always searching for better ways to deliver the new medium to viewers.

Dalt LeMasurier would die in a tragic mountaintop plane crash in 1957, three years after his television station went on the air.

Initially, the station was affiliated with the National Broadcasting Company, but in 1956 switched to the Columbia Broadcasting System. Channel 3 quickly became a key news and entertainment station for a region that covers a large portion of three states, but visitors who stopped in were somewhat startled, and a trifle disillusioned, by the reality of Duluth television in the black-and-white days.

"Most visitors came with a mental picture of a grand, magical wonderland where television programs were created," Marsh says with a smile. "What they saw was a cramped place with people walking sideways to get around. When I look at today's TV studios, like our present Broadcast Center, I scratch my head and wonder how we ever put out a picture or a radio signal from the Bradley Building."

KDLH's first home was a radio station converted into television studios, crowded with engineers, technicians, producers and directors tripping over each other in a tiny control room jammed with electronics.

Marsh shared office space with the continuity department on the radio side. The route to the station's only Associated Press teletype printer was a tortuous path that wound through the control room and the main TV studio, past the dressing rooms to the newsroom presided over by news director Bill Krueger. "It was like running an obstacle course to get a show together," Marsh says, "especially on a night when we were trying to collect scores and game results before air time."

By today's standards the studio was a relic.

"It would have been nearly impossible to do color from there because it was too small for the additional lights and other equipment that color requires," Marsh says, tossing an old photograph across the coffee table as Exhibit A.

Donn Larson, who was then television production manager, remembers:

"One of the big impediments to good production in that studio was the low ceiling. Lighting, even for black-and-white, was a real problem. Marsh, with his blond hair and large brown eyes, was particularly difficult to light.

"Of course, in those days, everything was live. There was no videotape yet. We used some film but, for the most part, commercials were set up and shot live in the studio, and we learned a lot of tricks just by doing. For instance, we found out that aerosol shaving cream was better than whipped cream for food commercials because it lasted longer under studio lighting conditions.

"The cameras were big and bulky. It was long before zoom lenses, and the cameraman would have to 'rack over'—turn the lens turret on the camera and focus—before the director punched it on. We had only two studio cameras, so while one was on, the other would be changing lenses and focusing."

Yet the makeshift TV studio was adequate for some novel programming.

"One of our regular weekly shows was Pee Wee Boxing in the studio," Larson recalls, "with Duluth Central Coach John Vucinovich as the host. The late Jim Lobb, our producer, built the ring, and little boys came in and boxed. The ring was portable, so we had to tear it down and set it up every week."

Larson remembers KDAL's first machine for film processing.

"It was a used KSTP reject, and a monster. It caused us a lot of grief. We'd have been better off to join forces with the other station to buy a first class processor we both could use. It was expensive, too. If it spoiled news film, that was bad enough. But when you spent all night filming a commercial and then lost it in the processor, that was costly. We'd just have to swallow our embarassment and go back and do it all over again."

The day-to-day boss was Odin S. Ramsland, a handsome,

gregarious commercial sales manager with a receding hairline, quick wit, magnetic personality and a legion of friends. The station operated with Dalt LeMasurier's business sense and Odin Ramsland's sales and managerial talent.

"When he was in New York, the ad reps and agencies would say, 'Ramsland's in town, be on your toes,'" Marsh recalls. "Even our competitors liked and respected Odin. He was shrewd but fair and always willing to listen if you had something bothering you. He never turned a deaf ear to the staff, and his door was always open. But when you asked for a raise, you got what we called his 'North Dakota arithmetic'—never as much as you thought you deserved, and often nothing at all. Sometimes you went away shaking your head and wondering what he'd said.

"He was an ideal boss. He kept in touch with everything that went on at the station. He came through several times a day, talked to everybody, made sure everything was working and you didn't need something. He was always fair with me. I have tremendous respect for Odin."

Chief Engineer Bob Dettman, whose electronic ingenuity was acknowledged throughout the industry, completed the KDAL ownership-management triumvirate.

"He was a technical engineering genius," Marsh declares. "He built the equipment, even the control room consoles. He designed our present Broadcast Center at 425 West Superior Street and it was built under his supervision. He also had a great deal to do with the design of the Arena-Auditorium (now the Duluth Entertainment Convention Center)—sightlines, electronics, things like that. He was an absolute master at making do with what was available. It was a good thing, too, because we never had enough equipment—we still don't—and we got by with hand-me-down, second-hand castoffs from somewhere else. Dettman could make it work and keep it working.

"I went head-to-head with Bob just once, shortly after we moved from the Bradley Building into Broadcast Center in 1968.

By that time, I was doing hockey remotes on KDAL-Radio, and we had a remote box that weighed about 80 pounds. It was about 15 by 15 by 12 inches and right out of the Stone Age. It contained a lot of electronic mysteries such as batteries, wires, resistors and other things I didn't understand—but Dettman did."

Rushing to catch buses and airplanes on hockey trips, Marsh was loaded down with the "black box," a bag of microphones, cables and other assorted gear, plus his own luggage. One day he asked Dettman if there were simple, compact and more portable equipment that would do the job of the black box. Typically, Dettman's answer was that the old remote box was "good equipment that worked just fine."

Marsh responded: "Bob, a Model-T Ford was good equipment that worked just fine, too, but you don't see many of them on the road anymore."

"It didn't do any good," Marsh says. "I hauled that antique around to every game in the league until shortly after the station was sold to WGN, Chicago. One day, Carl Meyer, their chief engineer, was here looking the place over, and he asked me what we used for remotes. I showed him the infamous black box. He said, 'I'll take care of that!' A few days later, a new one arrived—used, but new to us. It was about the size of a cigar box and weighed a fraction of the old one we'd been using. Dettman never said a word, but I think he always suspected I instigated the change."

Marsh settled in at the Bradley Building as sports director for both radio and television and, like the other air talent, he was expected to pull a regular staff announcer's radio shift "on the board," making station-break announcements, reading spots and occasionally spinning records.

"For a year and a half, every Sunday, I had a split shift. I put the station on the air at 7 a.m. and worked the board 'til noon, when Carl Casperson came in. He hosted the very lucrative, commercial-laden Serenade to a Sunday, a nice, easy-music program that ran from noon 'til five. Then, I came back on the board to work 'til midnight.

"Sunday morning always started with Reverend Arnold Anderson's sermon—live from the studio—in Finnish [he was with the Apostolic Lutheran Church in Esko]. That was a heck of a way to wake up, to that Finnish sermon! A half-hour recorded program would follow, then he'd come back on again, this time in English. About 9:30, we had a live pickup from a church and another [from First Lutheran in Duluth] at 11. Sandwiched in between was the Mormon Tabernacle Choir from KSL in Salt Lake—all in English, thank goodness.

"I was always there on time to open the place up. But, inevitably, one Sunday I overslept. There I was, at seven o'clock, driving towards downtown Duluth at about 45 miles an hour, and the radio station came on the air, right on time, with the national anthem. When it was over, Reverend Anderson came on in Finnish. He'd been doing that program every Sunday since the world began and, that day, when I didn't show up in time, he signed the station on the air himself. There really wasn't much to it—just check in by phone with the transmitter engineer down on Park Point and flip a couple of switches."

Even with the routine, the staffer had to be on his toes.

"You never took anything for granted. The Sunday church remotes were set up in advance. At the studio, we'd just patch the remote line into the patch board, turn up the gain [volume control] and listen on the line for any unusual background noise. One Sunday, I turned up the pot [the dial that controls the gain] and heard organ music, so I knew I had the church connection.

"Suddenly, two guys were talking on the line. One guy asks, 'Hey, Ed, you got a organ there?' The other guy says, 'Hell, no! I ain't got no damn organ!' A private line had inadvertently been patched in our line to First Lutheran. I had only a couple of minutes to straighten that out before the church service came on.

I called the phone company and told 'em, 'Our connection to First Lutheran isn't exactly our line!' They fixed it with only seconds to spare. Those two clowns on the phone were almost famous!"

Marsh was back on the board Monday through Friday, noon to three o'clock, in addition to doing the sportscasts on both radio and television.

Working the board, or "booth announcing," is living with the constant demands of myriad details: the program log, a schedule of live and recorded spot announcements, music cues, turntables and tape decks and the board itself: an intimidating console of pots, meters, switches and colored lights. Interruptions and distractions vie for the announcer's attention. Timing is in seconds, always controlled by an unforgiving clock. A 30-second station ID is just that—30 seconds—not an eyeblink longer or shorter; although most continuity writers will try to cram a little more commercial copy into it.

"It's like trying to pack 10 pounds of stuff into a five-pound sack," Marsh says with a grin.

But, on the whole, the morning and afternoon board shifts on weekdays were a breeze, largely because those were the waning days of the radio soap operas: *Ma Perkins, One Man's Family, Life Can be Beautiful, The Romance of Helen Trent* and the like. The daily quarter-hour continuing dramas got their nickname from the fact that most were sponsored by soap makers. All four radio networks (CBS, NBC, ABC and Mutual) carried them, and they provided important revenue for the affiliates.

"We rode CBS all afternoon with station breaks every 15 minutes, 'til about three o'clock, when we'd go local again," Marsh recalls. "I hadn't been in Duluth long enough to really know how fast the weather can change. With a wind shift off the big lake, you can swelter one minute and freeze the next. One day, I gave the temperature at one o'clock as 55 degrees. Fifteen minutes later, I hit the mike for a station break, looked at the thermometer and said, 'The temperature downtown is . . . Holy Cow! It's dropped to 40!' I got a few calls on that."

Anchoring radio news at noon and early evening was Bill Krueger, then dean of Twin Ports news broadcasters. His deep-voiced reporting, laced with keen analysis, gradually built the largest, most loyal audience in the region. Before retiring in 1985, Krueger's writing and broadcast talents, plus his journalistic integrity and professionalism, would bring him an impressive list of honors.

Marsh's first sportscast of the day was on radio at about 5:30 p.m., "right in the middle of the time I was getting my show together for the six o'clock TV news block," he recalls. "Late weekday afternoons were pretty hectic."

The television news team at six was headed by the versatile Dick Anthony, a long time KDAL personality, followed by Gordy Paymar with the weather and Marsh's sports, all squeezed into a quarter-hour. Earl Henton succeeded Krueger at 10 and anchored that show.

Henton already was a fixture in Duluth broadcasting. Before coming to KDAL as program director in 1953, his 10 p.m. radio news on WEBC, sponsored by Minnesota Power & Light Company, was unrivaled. He and announcer Ade Carlson ("Reddy Kilowatt reminds you that the things you do electrically are done with speed, with accuracy and with downright economy") were the last radio voices thousands of Northern Minnesota listeners heard each night before bedtime. Broadcasting over the Arrowhead Network, a three-station hookup consisting of WEBC, WMFG Hibbing and WHLB Virginia, Henton at 10 o'clock held up well in the region, even against the legendary Cedric Adams, whose folksy newscast from Minneapolis beamed into the northland on WCCO's clear channel 830 frequency.

"On television, too, Earl was unbeatable," Marsh says. "No other station in the Twin Ports was ever a serious competitor for his 10 o'clock TV news on Channel 3. His ratings were consistently high. Anthony at six was equally dominant."

It was fast company for the new kid on the block, the youngster with the big eyes, blond crewcut and machine-gun delivery.

"The time slot was really tight, with a total of only 15 minutes for the news, weather and sports," Marsh says. "Out of that total, you had to subtract time for the commercials. But, it's funny. Now, we have a half hour but we still don't seem to have any more time. Sometimes it seems I have less time now for my TV sports now than I did 30 years ago when the whole package ran only 15 minutes."

Marsh's first play-by-play broadcast on KDAL Radio was of a UMD hockey game during the 1960-61 season and originated from the Duluth Curling Club on London Road under conditions that could only be regarded as primitive.

"The building's gone now," he says. "Space was limited, so it was always jammed. The Bulldogs played St. Thomas College the first night and the Port Arthur Juniors on Saturday. I was right in the crowd, above one of the exits. We didn't have a broadcast booth or even a table—literally held the equipment on our laps, or set it on the floor. For later games, we rigged up a board shelf about 10 feet long and a foot wide and balanced all our gear and papers on that."

In the next season, his first hockey road trip for KDAL included a 650-mile ride in the team bus across Michigan's Upper Peninsula, across the Mackinac bridge and down to East Lansing.

"It was the northern route and took 23 hours," Marsh recalls. "By the time we got there, I didn't feel much like broadcasting, and the team didn't feel much like playing. Luckily, we had a day to recover before the game."

Marsh has probably seen more Western Collegiate Hockey Association games than anyone—except perhaps Lee Bohnet, former sports information director at the University of North

Dakota, or Tom Greenhoe of Michigan Tech and later of the Minnesota Sports Information Department.

In his nearly 40 years at the mike, Marsh broadcast from buildings that are no longer with us: the venerable Duluth Curling Club, Houghton's Dee Stadium, the "Potato Barn" in Grand Forks.

"Some of them were all-purpose buildings, not specifically designed for sports events," Marsh says. "The Potato Barn was an old World War II Quonset hut. The broadcast booth was so small I had to stand. There wasn't room to sit. But it was warm—they furnished a heater. Sometimes, it was colder inside the Potato Barn than it was outside. And, that rink! It usually had 'snirt'—a combination of snow and dirt—on the ice because the Quonset hut had cracks in it. That Dakota wind could really kick up the prairies.

"In Houghton, the one good thing about Dee Stadium was that it was only a couple of blocks from the hotel, the Douglas House. On some winter nights, that was a blessing. The Douglas House—we called it the Doghouse—had a coiled rope in each room on the upper floors. One end was tied to the radiator and, in case of fire, you tossed the other end out the window. That was your fire escape. Of course, with the huge snowfalls Upper Michigan gets every year, you really didn't need a fire escape. You could just step out a second-story window into a snowbank!

"The booth in Dee Stadium was up high on one end of the rink. When the play was at the other end of the ice, we couldn't see much. Later on, when Bob Junkert started broadcasting games for WDSM, he could see even less because he didn't have enough seniority to get inside in the booth. They put him on top of the box, under the rafters, and the billowing American flag kept getting in his face."

Every road trip was an adventure. Marsh recalls one aromatic game in Denver.

"D-U Arena had been condemned, so it was closed for refurbishing. Special events, including Denver hockey, were being held in the Denver Coliseum. A couple of days before, they'd had a big western cattle show in there, and it took days for the place to air out. It was ripe enough to clear your sinuses."

D-U Arena eventually went back in service with a varicolored interior. "Believe this or not, the walls are deep purple," Marsh says. "It's a nightmare for goalies."

Within a year or so of his arrival at KDAL, Marsh was broadcasting not only UMD hockey games on a fairly regular basis, but also high school football, hockey and basketball in a schedule of some 70 or 80 sports events a year.

Nobody in Duluth was yet doing remote television.

"We simply didn't have the facilities," Marsh says. "Radio was pretty simple: a remote box, a couple of microphones, a leased phone line back to the transmitter and we were on the air. TV required a lot more."

Television remotes came shortly after KDAL was sold in 1959 to WGN Continental Broadcasting, the radio-television arm of the *Chicago Tribune* empire—the call letters WGN representing the *Tribune's* modest claim to being the "World's Greatest Newspaper." WGN assumed active management in 1960, with no changes in KDAL's existing personnel. The ownership would last for the next 19 years.

Not long after the change, WGN provided KDAL's television mobile broadcast unit, the first in the Twin Ports. It consisted of an old Dodge van the size of a laundry truck, along with three remote cameras with wooden tripods, sync generator, cables, video monitors, microphones and attendant electronic equipment. Steel racks held everything neatly and securely inside. Bob Dettman went to work to make it operational. Within a few months, it was painted white, lettered "KDAL Television" and ready to go.

"It was ponderous equipment compared to today's electronics," recalls Bruce Nimmo, then an engineer-cameraman assigned to the unit. "Everything was vacuum tubes; no microchips or transistors in those days."

There was one condition attached to WGN's largess: the mobile unit must be used for church telecasts. All other uses were to be secondary.

"We did the church remotes according to a regular formula based on denomination," Nimmo recalls. "Jim Lobb, our director, was a great organizer. We'd do services from one church three times in a row, then rotate to another for two or three telecasts. We covered both Duluth and Superior, and even did a show from a spiritualist church once."

With the cooperation of the Duluth school system, the unit also did live telecasts from schools, often outdoors.

"We had three microwave antennae," Nimmo remembers. "The sender on the remote unit, another on the transmitter tower and one on the roof of the Bradley Building—so we could shoot at either location from the truck. The outside shows attracted a lot of attention. With the microwave dish right on the ground, we'd have to make sure kids didn't walk in front of it and block the signal to the transmitter. That would knock us off the air, and it never failed to happen."

One remote sports event didn't require the use of the mobile unit, but did take a good deal of muscle, speed and luck: professional wrestling matches live, before a studio audience. The studio and the audience were next door to the Bradley Building, on the second floor of the Knights of Columbus Hall.

"In the early days of television, wrestling was a popular staple," Marsh says. "Harvey Solon of Duluth was promoting pro wrestling in Northern Minnesota then, and he worked a deal with the station to broadcast a weekly show in Duluth.

"We scheduled the shows to start at 10:45 p.m., a half-hour

after the news block went off, and it was a real scramble to get everything set up. A filmed show came on after the news-weather-sports, while the engineers and cameramen dismantled the cameras, hauled them downstairs to the street, over to the KC Hall and up more stairs to where the ring was set up. They had less than 30 minutes to get everything working and, many times, it was touch and go."

Bruce Nimmo was one of the cameramen who performed the weekly miracle:

"Luckily, we had enough coaxial cable for a sort of permanent link. We ran it out a window and across a fire escape from the Bradley Building to the KCs and left it there. The cameras came apart, so Skip Newburg, George Gothner and I would haul them over first, then go back for the big triangular aluminum dolly. We mounted one camera on that, on the floor, right in the crowd. The other was on a wooden tripod and we carried it into the balcony. That tripod was almost as heavy as the camera."

Marsh did the ringside commentary.

"When I got the assignment, I didn't know very much about professional wrestling, so I had a few talk sessions with Harvey and two top wrestlers of the day, Verne Gagne, a former University of Minnesota football star, and Wilbur Snyder. They briefed me on just about everything I needed to know and told me to pick up the rest as I went along."

Some 200 tickets were given away to assure the shows a noisy, enthusiastic audience. The bouts were an instant success and ran for nearly two years on the air. They also opened another door for Marsh.

"One of the biggest names in televised wrestling was Marty O'Neill in the Twin Cities, who worked for Verne Gagne's production at the time. When videotape came in, they'd tape 16 or 20 bouts over a weekend and send the tapes out to a dozen or so subscriber stations around the country. Marty's wrestler interviews between bouts promoted upcoming shows in towns around the circuit.

"Shortly after we stopped doing live wrestling in Duluth, Harvey and Gagne asked me to fill in for Marty, who was out of action for several weeks with dental surgery.

"I was paid very well, but it was one of the toughest jobs I ever had. The guys were great, but the grind was a killer. We taped as many as 65 interviews in an afternoon. The pitch was pretty standard: 'The good guy is going to meet the bad guy in the bout of the century in two weeks in your town and you better be there to see the slaughter.' We started about noon and didn't stop 'til after six and I had to keep track of who was fighting who in what town and when."

A sports purist though he may be, Marsh has respect and admiration for the wrestlers.

"Professional wrestling is an entertainment. It's different from college and high school wrestling, which is a true sport. Pro wrestlers are superb athletes, many of them former college football players. Whatever you might think, they do get hurt sometimes, but not often, because they're in absolutely top physical shape and know their business. They're real troupers. When that red light goes on, their characters change and they go into action. I always enjoy being with them."

He remembers, in particular, one of the Monday night shows in the Duluth KC Hall.

"Gene Kiniski was a bad guy at the time, a real heel. People would work up a genuine hate for Gene. They called him 'Big Thunder.' That night, he wrestled Wilbur Snyder, who was always a hero type and a crowd favorite. I was announcing ringside and, as part of the show, Gene was giving me a bad time during the bout. Next day, he and I were having lunch at the Flame Restaurant down on the waterfront. We were about to order when a guy came over, stopped, and looked hard at Gene and then over at me. Gene smiled at him and said hello. The guy just stuck his finger in Gene's face and said, 'How can you sit here with Marsh Nelson? Last night you threatened to tear his head off!'

"Gene said, 'Hey, when I'm out of the ring, I'm a normal person just like you and everybody else! I like good food and good friends!'

"Another night—remember, these were live broadcasts—Kiniski got in hot water with Verne Gagne. The wrestling show was sponsored by Gera-Speed, a vitamin supplement Gagne owned and promoted on the show. Gene threw his opponent out of the ring onto the floor, leaped the ropes and continued the match out in the crowd. He picked the poor guy up, twirled him around a couple of times and tossed him into Gagne's vitamin display. Bottles flew everwhere! There were pills all over the place. Gagne was fit to be tied. The crowd loved it!"

Another of Marsh's wrestling friends was the villainous Doctor X, who hid his identity behind a black skin-tight mask over his head. The bad "Doctor" was easy to hate. He was cast as a cheating, unsportsmanlike bully. At least that's the way the fans saw him. Marsh knew him as he really was.

"His name was Dick Byers and he'd played football for Syracuse University. He was really a gentle, polite man out of the ring, but I could never convince my mother and dad of that. They used to say, 'You watch out for him. He's a bad guy!'

"Dick went to Japan for a series of exhibition bouts and, when he came back, he brought me a watch. Next time I visited the folks, Dad asked about the watch and I told him it was a gift from Doctor X. Dad was impressed. He thought a minute and said, 'Well, Son, I guess he's not such a bad man after all!'"

Marsh smiles. "Maybe there's some kind of lesson there. Things and people aren't always what they appear to be."

*Marsh's dad in 1918:*
*Pvt. Charles Nelson*

*Charlie Nelson and uncles Elmer*
*Gustafson and Roy Sjoberg*
*enjoyed bountiful hunting on the*
*Vermilion*
*River rice beds in 1925.*

*Marsh's dad in 1929:*
*Charlie and Peggy*

*Marsh's dad in 1938:*
*Police Chief*
*Charles Nelson*

*Gridiron heroes in 1945: Jim Keranen (No. 20), Don Avikainen and Marsh*

*Against a background unique to Minnesota's Iron Range, Marsh kicks from the hold of Ernie Mustonen in 1946.*

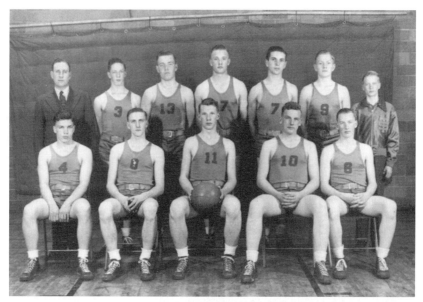

*Coach Mike Weinzierl, No. 9 Marsh Nelson and the 1946
Region 7 basketball champs of Tower-Soudan High School*

*Marsh risked his high school eligibility to play for the V-8's.*

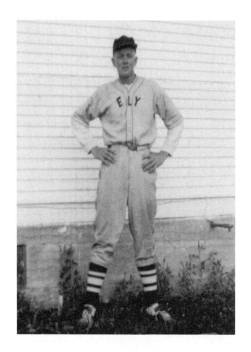

*'Big Train' Nelson, 1949*

*Marsh and a couple of pals were among hundreds of hopefuls in 1949 at the Giants spring camp.*

RUSS BERG

*The Fourth of July, 1951, meant baseball: Marsh caught for the Tower Colts, 'Bunker' Hill umpired and H.H. Stevens went to bat for the opposition.*

*Marsh's Macalaster days meant hockey.*

T.J. ABERCROMBIE

*In 1954 the U.S. Army greeted another Pvt. Nelson.*

*By 1960 the Northland could put a face with the name:* **Marsh** *means* sp

RSH NELSON

*Sports!*

KDAL · RADIO

door Adv Co

*In 1961 the Vikings' general manager Bert Rose;*
*the coach was the fiery Stormin' Norman Van Brocklin.*

---

*The deep voice of Bob Junkert, a bowling teammate*
*in 1963, also was well known to Duluth-Superior fans.*

*Channel 3 beamed Marsh into thousands of homes.*

*In the company of legends: Marsh with John Mariucci, Bronco Nagurski, John Norlander.*

*In the early '70s commercials were still live.*

---

*In 1970 Marsh was still playing hockey and still had his crewcut, but Bobo "Toothless" Thomas was sans choppers.*

*The Nelson Collection, circa 1970:*
*Jo-Jo Vatalaro, Marsh, Harvey Solon,*
*Bill Cortes, Mike Radakovich*

———————————

*Marsh works a Vikings game in Met Stadium*
*with Dan Gleason.*

*Between Mertz and Betty Mortorelli, the driving forces*
*of UW-Superior athletics, at an alumni dinner in 1971*

---

*On the Channel 3 set in 1973*
*with Gordy Paymar, Bill Krueger and Ron Dehart*

*An October 1978 football road trip came to a crashing halt.*

*With Jim Finks, New Orleans general manager, in 1989*

*With Jack Buck of CBS and ex-Viking Bill Brown*

*Marsh Nelson, Tower-Soudan Class of 1946,
interviews Joel McDonald, Chisholm Class of 1991—the
all-time leading scorer in Minnesota high school basketball.*

# CHAPTER SEVEN

# Enter the Comb

Mary Jo White is a 30-year veteran of Channel 3, and as a television writer and producer she has influenced more than one on-air personality. In Marsh Nelson's case, she changed an entire image with the sweep of a 39-cent comb.

For years, Marsh's trademark was a bush crewcut, an inch-long towhead flattop that stood straight up. That changed one afternoon in 1970 in the station lunchroom.

"I happened to walk in for a cup of coffee," Mary Jo recalls, "and Marsh was sitting there with Hunter Como from the radio side. It was shortly after we'd moved from the Bradley Building into Broadcast Center—I remember, because the carpets were still clean!

"Marsh rubbed his hand across his head and said to Hunter, 'I gotta get a haircut.' I looked at him. His crewcut was getting shaggy.

"Suddenly, I had a brainstorm. I said, 'Marsh, don't move,' and ran to get my comb. He sat still while I combed his hair and parted it on one side. With a little spray, it stayed down. I swept it around his forehead, and the effect was almost unbelievable!"

Other station staffers who wandered into the lunchroom thought so, too.

"I think Marsh was flattered," she says, "and I told him to try it on the air that night, just to see the public reaction. He wasn't on camera more than a minute when the phones started ringing, and they kept ringing all evening. It was unanimous. Everybody said, 'Keep the hair!'"

Former television news director Ron Lund remembers:

"Crewcuts went out in the late 1950s, and Marsh's stood out like a sore thumb. Even after Mary Jo finally convinced him to grow it out, it seemed to take forever to make the transition."

But the crewcut was history. Marsh never changed Mary Jo's original hair style.

"I never realized people cared that much about appearance, or a small thing like a hairdo," he says with a shake of his head. "It dies hard, though. That was more than 20 years ago, and people still ask me about the crewcut. I tell 'em, 'The crew bailed out!'"

Marsh learned the power of the medium on another occasion:

"It was on a fishing trip with Warren Kregness of the Tower Bank and Doctor Dick Dobbs of Duluth. They owned a rustic cabin up there in the wilds of Canada—the only one on the island—and we had to fly there in Warren's plane.

"It was before videotape and I took a 16-millimeter Bell and Howell movie camera along and shot some footage of the fish we caught. When I got back, I used some of the film on my sports show and made an off-hand reference to the cabin as the 'Hope Lake Hilton.' I didn't use any names except to mention the 'Tower banker.'

"A lot of people saw the show and at least two took it seriously. A couple of guys from the Twin Cities made calls to Tower, looking for 'the banker.' The operator connected them with

Warren. They both wanted reservations at the Hope Lake Hilton. Warren hadn't seen the show and didn't know what they were talking about."

To a host of friends and co-workers at the station, Marsh is Marsh, an individualist who's preoccupied with his commitment to his profession, often to the exclusion of more mundane matters such as wardrobe, conversation around him and the demands of the clock. Either in spite of some personal idiosyncrasies or because of them, Marsh has endeared himself to the station's television production staff.

Consider a wintry December day several years ago.

"We were getting a fairly substantial snowfall all day," Ron Lund recalls. "About five o'clock in the afternoon, LaForge [General Manager John LaForge] came through and told everybody the station had made reservations for the staff across the street at the Radisson. Marsh got into his car, drove home in the snow, packed a bag and drove back down again."

In the past, Marsh's sport coats were the bane of camera operators and directors.

"Some of them were terrible," Lund says, "particularly the reds. Reds are bad on the air. The color bleeds on camera. He had one that was a real problem. We'd hide it. We even threatened to burn it. We sent him out to buy a new one, and he came back with another red one.

"Another of his jackets that gave directors fits was lemon yellow. It reflected the lights back into the camera, and the automatic iris tends to close down when it gets too much light."

TV operations manager Ken Flannery remembers his favorite Marsh sport coat. "It was like a horse blanket—red stripes and blue-black plaid. I don't know what it is about sportscasters, they all love plaids. It might make a good test pattern to focus on, but it's hell on camera."

With maturity came a more conservative wardrobe. Lund credits the feminine influence.

"Judy improved his color coordination a hundred percent," he says. "We even talked about bringing her down on the set to fix his hair. It isn't that he doesn't care about things like that. It's just that he's got other things on his mind. He's better about it now."

Unlike many news and sports anchors, Marsh writes all of his own copy.

"Marsh probably types more than anybody else at the station," says Lund, "so I tried to make it easier for him by getting him an electronic typewriter. Marsh and electronics are incompatible. For the first few days, there were fights in that little office between Marsh and the new typewriter. I don't know how he managed it, but he'd get the ribbon wound around the daisy wheel. We'd straighten it out but, in a day or so, the same thing would happen.

"He's death on typewriters. He hits the keys so hard the fonts—the characters—come loose from the type bars and go flying through the air. Since we use a certain kind of print in news scripts, I was down on my hands and knees picking up type and sticking it back on. Finally, we gave him back his old manual."

Marsh's personal shorthand system can be an unbreakable code to anyone unfamiliar with it. "Chicken scratches on a typewriter," Lund calls it with a smile. "He has most of the script in his head, with a few key words, phrases and numbers on paper. Nobody else can read it."

Earl Henton, for many years the news anchor on Channel 3, recalls a night when he unexpectedly faced a Marsh Nelson sports script with no warning.

"I forget why Marsh wasn't there. I'd just finished the news when they handed me his script and told me to do it. It looked like Egyptian hieroglyphics, and just as intelligible."

There are times when working with Marsh can be hectic and frustrating. Getting him on the air on time, especially on television, is a challenge.

"He doesn't pre-plan," says Lund. "Everything is last-minute. We almost gave up trying to get him on the set for the opening shot with the other anchors at the beginning of the show. Marsh lives in his own world."

Perhaps it's a legacy from the KSTP days with Dick Nesbitt, but Marsh crams every second before air time, trying to get the latest news into his programs. This usually puts the crunch on his colleagues. Says Lund:

"He doesn't start writing much of his 6:20 sports 'til after 5 because he wants to see what's coming down the line on the network feed, in case there's something he can use. So, we search the video on two one-hour tapes for the stuff he needs, edit it, dub it off and get it into the tape order for the control room. We're cutting pieces for his show while the news is on the air. Many of Marsh's tapes go upstairs piecemeal.

"For the 10, the national satellite feed starts at 8:45. Marsh goes on at the end of the show, so we have to find what he wants and get it upstairs before he calls for it on the air. Sometimes we don't make it. If you've ever watched, you've seen the looks he gives when a video clip doesn't show up on cue. He used to make comments on the air. Now, it's just those looks."

Yet Marsh can be methodical and stoutly resist changes that might upset his established routine, whether it's his set number of situps each night before bed, his workout at the YMCA three days a week—or the clutter in his office.

A corridor divides the television station from KDAL Radio, now totally separate from and independent of Channel 3. Just off the TV newsroom is Marsh's closet-size office where every square inch of wall space is covered with photos, posters, buttons, ribbons, schedules, yellowed newspaper clippings, awards and citations and a stack of commemorative hockey pucks on his desk.

He has to squeeze past a filing cabinet and slide files to get to the creaking swivel chair on the working side of his desk.

Lund recalls: "Department heads held periodic inspection tours of the station to pinpoint messy areas. John LaForge led the parade, and nobody was exempt. There's no cure for Marsh's office. When we put new carpets in everything had to be removed, and we figured that when he put it back together Marsh would clean it up, get all the junk out of there. No way. When the carpet job was done, he put it all back very carefully, just the way it came out: scattered newspapers, magazines, record books from the time of the Great Flood, stacks of slides, pictures, tapes. The only thing missing was the dust."

Marsh has his own style.

"Nobody knows what hours he keeps, because he comes and goes all day," Lund recalls from his days at the station. "He's like the wind. He appears and disappears. But he's a joy to work with because he's a real pro.

"He's one of the best ad libbers in the business, and his sense of timing is uncanny. If you're producing a commercial with him, he's great. He can walk in, glance at the script and the producer will tell him, 'Marsh, we gotta do this in 30 seconds, or 60 seconds, or whatever.' He'll do it. The first time. No retakes. Every time. On live special events like the Beargrease [sled dog race] or Grandma's Marathon, all you have to do is turn Marsh loose, tell him how much time he has, and he'll hit it, right to the second. He never misses."

Rik Jordan recalls the day a Soviet hockey team came to town.

"The Gorky Torpedoes. It was in 1980 and they beat UMD soundly that night. They held a news conference in the Radisson about five o'clock that afternoon, before the game. The Russian interpreters all had big coats and black hats and looked like KGB, there to make sure nobody wandered off or said something unauthorized.

"They gave us a list of their players who'd be on that night.

The names were impossible. Marsh looked at the list and just kinda whistled to himself.

"I could hardly believe it. By the time the game started at seven, Marsh had memorized all those Russian names and the numbers—with the proper pronunciations. In less than two hours. I'd never seen that before. Hockey is one of the toughest sports to do play-by-play because the player lines change so fast and so often, but I've never seen Marsh use a score sheet to do a hockey game. He just doesn't make many mistakes but, the rare times he does, he covers up nicely."

KDAL announcer Kerry Rodd, a former Cloquet athlete, succeeded Marsh as the radio voice of UMD hockey. Jordan, who shared the play-by-play booth with Marsh for years, and still does color for Rodd on home games, looked back on the day the change came.

"I think Marsh was relieved. He can spend more time at home now. The way he and Judy are going, they'll be honeymooning for the next 10 years. He has time for the things he likes: grouse hunting, duck hunting, fishing—things that had had to take second place to the hockey schedule from fall to spring.

"Road games are a grind—every Thursday, Friday, Saturday and Sunday. Once in awhile, you get a weekend series at home, then you're off again the following Thursday. I don't think the average person understands what that's like. Marsh likes to travel but after 29 years, it finally got to him. I don't like travel, and it ate me up.

"But, he's a tough act to follow. As Kerry himself put it, how do you replace a legend? It's a little like Les Steckel replacing Bud Grant at the Vikings or Bart Starr following Lombardi with the Packers. You're really under the microscope. But Marsh is a pro. He helped Kerry through the transition, showed him some of the tricks he'd learned the hard way over the years. I don't think very many people know that."

Jordan came to KDAL Radio in 1978 from a Mankato station.

"Marsh is known all over the state," he says, "even in southern Minnesota. When I started working with him on hockey, I knew he wasn't going to adapt to my style; I'd have to fit into his. For the first few games, I just sat there and, at the right time, I'd say, 'That's right, Marsh, great play!' He never told me what to do or say or what he expected from me. We just started working together. When he'd look at me I'd say something and hope it was intelligent."

Jordan delights in telling of their first few nights together in the Arena broadcast booth.

"I'm blind in one eye. Caught a hockey puck in the eye in high school. I couldn't see him on my left side. When he threw me a hand cue, I didn't know it unless I was looking at him, or unless the buttons on his sleeve jingled. Finally, I asked if I could sit on his right side. When I explained the problem, he was really touched, and maybe a little embarrassed. He grinned, patted me on the shoulder in that way he has with people he likes, and said, 'Is that all? I thought you were just stupid!' We switched positions and got along just fine."

At 61, Marsh is in top physical condition and works hard to stay that way. "He's a health nut, and that's good, but sometimes it's interesting if you room with him on the road," Jordan says. "Every night before bed, it's 35 or 40 situps in his pajamas. When you do situps, you kinda inch along. He starts on one end of the room and ends up on the other, scooting along the floor.

"He's a cheap date. On the road for KDAL, he'll come back and turn in an expense voucher of 25 dollars—for all three days! He eats hamburgers, and never parties. One time we flew to Boston for a UMD-Providence game. Marsh had reserved a rental car—naturally, the cheapest he could get, some sub-compact for $19 a day. When we got to Logan Airport, the clerk didn't have the car he'd rented. Instant panic. He told her we had to have a car to get to a hockey broadcast.

"'Will you accept a little bigger car for the same price?' she asked. Marsh allowed as how that would be OK, and she made a couple of phone calls. Finally she told somebody named 'Billy' it was an emergency, to get a car over right away. It turned out to be a Cadillac Fleetwood Brougham. She said, 'We're sorry, sir, but will this be acceptable? Same price?' We drove that Caddy all over Boston that weekend for $19 a day, gas included!

"There's one very important thing about Marsh that some younger kids in this business don't understand," Jordan says. "This guy doesn't have to prove anything. He's played every sport he talks about. He's like a walking sports encyclopedia."

Marsh is in constant demand as a speaker and rarely declines an invitation to appear in public—be it master of ceremonies at a high school athletic banquet, riding a parade float or hosting a benefit performance. He never prepares for a speech and never uses notes. The format is always the same: five minutes of opening commentary, followed by a free-wheeling, no-holds-barred, question-answer, give-and- take with the audience. He's never stumped by a question and revels in frank, plain-talk evaluation of sports, teams and individual athletes. He leaves no doubt where he stands on a given issue.

"He's not like a lot of guys in broadcasting—egoists who just want to be on the air," says Rik Jordan. "Marsh really knows what he's talking about, because he's been there. I respect that. If he tells a radio audience about a tough body check, or a great play, you can believe it."

Bruce Bennett of the *Duluth News-Tribune* puts it this way:

"He's not part of the jock culture that's permeated radio and TV sports, but he was a good athlete in high school and college. In my opinion, over the years, Marsh has become one of the leading hockey broadcasters in the nation. He combines the enthusiasm of a fan with the knowledge of a professional. No. 1:

he's a friend of mine. No. 2: he's a competitor of mine in the sports business. I can tell you, he's great at both."

UMD hockey coach Mike Sertich:

"He's fair and balanced. He calls them as he sees them, which is what a good reporter does. He has a great overall love for the game and sports in general. He's played himself, so he understands the game and the players."

Rik Jordan remembers his first meeting with Marsh:

"I was working at KOZY in Grand Rapids [Minnesota] back in the late 1960s. We needed a banquet speaker for our monthly Sports Boosters' banquet and somebody suggested Marsh Nelson. I'd heard him on radio and seen him on TV, but I'd never met him. When he showed up, he went around and talked to everybody and passed out a questionnaire asking what people in Itasca County wanted to see on television sports. He was interested in people and friendly with everybody. I thought to myself, 'What a phony! Nobody can really be that nice!' I was wrong. Three years later, I was working shoulder to shoulder with him and I can tell you, he *really is* that nice.

"Often, when we were doing home hockey games, my wife would be working and I'd bring the kids down to the press box with me. Marsh was their hero. He treated them as real people, not babies.

"He's never lost that small-town touch. He has friends in all walks of life, all levels of society, including many people who are less fortunate. He loves kids and senior citizens, celebrities and just plain folks. To Marsh, there's no distinction. If he's your friend, he's your friend. Period."

CHAPTER EIGHT

# Mishaps

S ome of the worst times in this business make some of the best memories," Marsh says, loading dinner plates into the dishwasher. "You never forget the embarassing moments." After nearly 40 years in broadcasting, Marsh Nelson has accumulated his share of embarassments.

"First, you learn early that every microphone is live, even if you think you know it isn't," he says with a grin.

Announcer Rik Jordan agrees. For 11 years, Jordan was Marsh's color commentator on KDAL's hockey radio broadcasts. He remembers in particular one UMD-Wisconsin game in Duluth.

"Wisconsin had a great team that year, and a great coach, Bob Johnson. Marsh and I were in the press box. Midway through the second period, the referee called a penalty. The Wisconsin players didn't like the call and their captain complained, long and loud. During the lull, we broke for a commercial and, when we got it back, the Badgers were still complaining. In fact, their captain drew a misconduct penalty for yelling at the ref.

"Play was at a standstill. Marsh and I kept the chatter going and, finally, Marsh said, 'You know, Rik, I think the guy's got a legitimate bitch.' In the next instant, he realized what he'd said. All I could say was, 'Yeah, I guess he does.' Now, 'bitch' is a word you hear a lot on television, but rarely if ever on radio, especially in a play-by-play broadcast. He just slid over it and kept talking. He covered it up so well that hardly anybody noticed, but we heard about it next day. I kept the tape all these years."

As the equipment got more sophisticated, live broadcasting got more treacherous.

"One night we were simulcasting a UMD hockey game on both radio and TV from North Dakota," Marsh recalls, "and our signal was carried by satellite from Grand Forks back to Duluth. You could pick up that signal anywhere in the country if you had the satellite coordinates. One year, 'Heatwave' [former Channel 3 meteorologist Richard Berler] picked up several of our games in Laredo, Texas.

"I forgot that even on a commercial break to the studio we were actually still on the air from North Dakota, because the mike was always open to the satellite. Anything we said during that commercial went out, too. On one of those breaks—when we weren't actually on the air—I happened to remark to my colleague, Walt Ledingham, 'Boy, I wish this period would end. I gotta go to the can.' Of course, that went out loud and clear, and a lot of people watching the game on satellite heard it.

"Hobey Baker Award winner [1983-84] Tommy Kurver was a Bulldog defenseman that year—he's now in the NHL. About a month after that broadcast, Tommy's mother met me on the street and said, 'Marsh, did you ever get to the can that night in Grand Forks?' That taught both Walt and me a lesson about open mikes.

"Another time, we were doing a game on radio from D-U Arena in Denver. Bob Schwartz, a long-time Bulldog fan, and Mike Radakovich—my color man and later assistant coach at

Colorado College—were in the broadcast booth with me. I had a lavalier mike on a cord around my neck so I could stand or sit to call the game, and we dangled a second mike over the press box rail to pick up crowd noise.

"Late in the second period, Denver's George Morrison got a little rough. It was totally out of character for him—he was so thin he didn't usually dare tangle with anybody. But something riled him that night, and he set his eye on UMD wing Cam Fryer. Morrison took seven or eight strides across the ice and stapled Fryer to the boards. Cam missed about a month of the remaining season.

"We're supposed to be impartial, but we're also human, and the three of us in the booth really got after Morrison. I shut off my neck mike for a moment, but forgot about the crowd mike hanging outside the box. When we leaned out, that mike picked up some of the most colorful press box language Northern Minnesota ever heard. Monday morning, the FCC [Federal Communications Commission] called Carl Casperson, our radio program director, and they were upset, to say the least."

Incidents can happen in the studio, too.

"You're really a slave to the electronics, the machinery," Marsh says. "One night, during my regular 10:20 sports, the right piece of film didn't come up on cue. I thought I was off camera and voiced a mild profanity, something like 'damn it!' You do something like that and you find out how many people are watching. Next day, skier Paul Vesterstein said, 'Don't let it bother you. It shows you're human.'"

Marsh takes a deep breath. "I sure hate to screw up just to prove I'm human."

Marsh has learned many lessons from experience.

"I make it a practice to be on the scene at least an hour and a half before we go on with a game. I've learned, the hard way, that a lot of things can and do go wrong—such as a leased phone line that's been disconnected or a hookup torn down. More than once, Bob Junkert from WDSM and I would be both doing the same football game from Public School Stadium in Duluth and we'd find our radio broadcast lines dead because somebody at the phone company had pulled a patch. I can still hear Junk saying, 'But it's a fulltime line! It's there for the season!'"

Sometimes, leaving early can be almost as bad as arriving late.

"I'll never forget the night Pat Cadigan created the 55-yard line. He and I were doing a high school football game in Superior. I did the first three quarters but had to leave for a studio show. Pat was to take the rest of the play-by-play, and he'd never done it before. Driving back to Duluth, I had the car radio on and was halfway across the Blatnik Bridge when I heard Pat say, 'He's at the 40-yard line . . . the 45 . . . the 50 . . . the 55 . . . .' I damn near drove off the bridge!"

In addition to "the-mike-is-always-live," radio's other unwritten law is: Dead air is more than embarassing; it's unforgivable.

"You guard against even a few seconds of dead air," Marsh says. "Those few seconds could be the time somebody's fiddling with the dial trying to find your station."

A surprise delay in the action—a baseball game held up by rain or something wrong in an arena—leaves the announcer hanging out to dry, with little or nothing to talk about.

"Moments like that, I remember the day at Macalester when Dick Enroth made me a 30-minute extemporaneous speech about a chair," he says.

"It was like that one night in Yost Fieldhouse in Ann Arbor. UMD was playing the University of Michigan. The weather was miserable—an ice and sleet storm had wrecked a lot of power lines. About the middle of the second period, the lights went out in the fieldhouse. Everything stopped.

"Luckily, sitting in the stands behind me was a former Michigan hockey All-American, Neal Celley from Eveleth. When he saw my predicament, he came over and sat down next to me. He grabbed the spare mike, and we rehashed every hockey player in the history of the Iron Range. Thanks to Neal's memory and experiences with some real hockey greats, people he played with, we had about an hour and 20 minutes of very colorful stories until they got the lights back on in the arena.

"Radio remotes on the road I usually worked alone. I'd hook up my equipment and go find a phone to call the station and used a stopwatch to set an exact time to go on, down to the second. With that one-way line, I couldn't hear the station, so I couldn't get a direct audio cue. I'd count down with the stopwatch and just start talking. From that moment I'd have it 'til I signed off with something like 'Good night from Boston,' or 'Good night from Ann Arbor.' Later, I worked out a cue system with the station, some code words, so the studio announcer could take it back for x-number of minutes while I caught my breath.

"Now we have a two-way Class A line, the best the phone company has, with a voice coupler so we can talk back and forth and switch to the station for fill."

Thousands of National Football League fans know Marsh as the stadium voice of the Minnesota Vikings, first at Metropolitan Stadium in Bloomington, now at the Hubert H. Humphrey Metrodome in Minneapolis. Twenty minutes before the opening kickoff, his "Good morning, ladies and gentlemen, this is Marsh Nelson, your stadium announcer" opens the activity at every home game.

Play-by-play sports is an unscripted, unpredictable, free-wheeling, unexplored territory where glitches lurk. Although Marsh has built a reputation for accuracy in his reporting, mistakes are inevitable.

Working the Vikings public address system is three hours of tension. If the announcer calls a wrong tackler or pass receiver, 60,000 people in the Dome catch the mistake.

His job with the Vikings started small, as a member of the team's statistics staff in 1962, and came about through Marsh's friendship with Ole Haugsrud of Duluth, one of the original Vikings owners, and former University of Minnesota halfback Billy Bye, who was the Viking's first business manager. The NFL franchise was new and the front office was organizing the press crew. Marsh spent three or four years in the statistics booth, passing along official yardage, statistics and information on injuries and penalties to the assembled reporters over a closed-circuit pressbox public-address system.

The Vikings' first stadium p.a. voice was already familiar to sports fans. Marsh's friend Bob Casey, the stadium announcer for the Minnesota Twins, was hired to do Vikings games as well.

"He went along fine for most of one season," Marsh says, "until one game when the Vikings were playing the Giants. There was a penalty on one play, an ineligible receiver downfield. Casey's announcement was 'The Giants are penalized for an *illegitimate* receiver downfield.' Everybody got a kick out of that except the National Football League officials. When the word got back to NFL headquarters, they thought Casey was making light of the league and asked the Vikings to get a new p.a. announcer."

Frank Buetel had the job for a couple of years, then it alternated among the local sports broadcasters. When the Vikings management decided to go with one permanent announcer, Marsh was picked.

"I suppose I had the inside track because I'd been doing the internal p.a., and I suspect they felt it was safer to choose somebody from out of town rather than pick one Twin Cities man and make the others mad."

Marsh loves the job and, from the beginning, has approached it with his usual enthusiasm and professionalism.

"Before every game, I used to go down to the referee's room two hours before the game to meet with the officials, like Jim Tunney and the late Tommy Bell, to get clear on signals. In those days, the p.a. announcer would explain the officials' hand signals to the crowd: offsides, holding, tripping, false starts."

Spending time with the officials before a game has paid off many times for Marsh. Duluth sports columnist Bruce Bennett wrote about one such occasion, which developed on a sunny afternoon in 1975 at Metropolitan Stadium in Bloomington. "The Vikings were in the process of demolishing the Chicago Bears," Bennett wrote in his column. "It was early in the second quarter and Minnesota already led 14-0. Ed Marinaro had gathered in a wing pass for a 12-yard gain and an apparent first down.

"Over the public address system came the words, 'Flag on the play.' As the multitudes wondered—whether it was holding against the Vikings, which would nullify the gain, or any of an assortment of calls against the Bears, which the Vikings might or might not prefer to a 12-yard gain, the p.a. man added: 'The penalty is against the Bears for an illegal cut.'"

Marsh was the p.a. announcer.

Bennett remembers, "Down the press row, a Chicago cynic piped up, 'What's this, a butcher shop? Some guy musta' got horse meat instead of U.S. prime!'"

Bennett's column resumed: "The penalty [was] declined but the confusion remained. A few plays later, on a Viking punt, the Bears were flagged for another illegal cut. By now, the Chicago press was in a quandary—'What's an illegal cut?' they demanded—but not Marsh Nelson."

Later, Marsh discussed it with Bennett:

"'That's a call against the defensive team for blocking a wide receiver below the waist before the ball is passed or punted. How did I know? I make it a point to go down and check with the officials before the game and go over their signals. When I saw the signal, a chopping motion with the hand in front of the knee, I recognized it.'"

"The illegal cut, a rare call, was new that day," Bennett wrote. "The fact that Nelson . . . was johnny-on-the-spot with the call and had done his homework is doubtless one reason he has the job and has kept it. . . . "

As everything else has, the job has changed over the years.

"Now I don't have to check signs ahead of time. The officials are wired, and they announce all the penalties from the field," Marsh says.

Not all the surprises were on the field. One of Marsh's favorite incidents occurred in an unlikely place.

"Met Stadium had a lavatory reserved for the news media right behind the press box. It was built in later years because the public washrooms were so far away and, on cold days, the public would crowd into the heads just to get warm. At halftime or just after a game it was a mad scramble, and the reporters just didn't have time to wait in line or fight the crowd. So we got our own latrine.

"One Sunday, by the time the half came, I was about to bust and headed for the latrine as soon as I could. There, standing outside the door, were a couple of Secret Service guys and a regular stadium usher. The Secret Service waved me off, but the usher said, 'He's OK. He's the stadium announcer. He's gotta go in there.'

"They gave me a pretty hard look, but let me in. There was only one man inside, standing at the urinal with his back to me. I stepped up beside him and proceeded to proceed. He looked over at my sweater, with the Vikings staff emblem on it, and said: 'I'm rooting for your team today. I've always been a fan of Bud Grant's Vikings.'"

It was Vice President Gerald Ford.

"We talked a few minutes and I told him I'd just been to Ann Arbor on a UMD hockey trip and had seen where he played football for the University of Michigan. His eyes lit up and he became quite friendly. He was happy to talk about the Wolverines—he might not have been as warm and friendly if I'd asked about foreign aid or the national debt.

"Conversations don't last long in the men's room, so when we finished what we were there for, I went back to the press box, and he was ushered away by the Secret Service. You meet the nicest people in the bathroom."

Marsh's present Vikings' booth companions are spotter Jeff Turtinen, Bruno Waldner, who runs the 30-second clock, and timekeeper Jack Dryer. They agree on at least one major irritation: the Vikings band.

"In Met Stadium, we had a cue for the band. The referee would signal a time out and I'd say, 'There's a time out on the field.' Harvey Solon always kidded me about that, too. He'd say, 'Where else would the time out be?' But, without my cue, the band wouldn't play.

"Now, in the Dome, the band is playing all the time. They're still playing when the team is calling plays, or breaking from the huddle. They must get paid by the note. If you're sitting in the stands, you never get a chance to chat with your friends because the band is blaring and the cheerleaders are jumping up and down. I don't believe we really need the sideshows. The crowd responds to what the people in the purple jerseys are doing, not to the band, the cheerleaders or a circus entertainer. They should spend the money for another good defensive back."

Since starting with the Vikings organization a quarter-century ago, Marsh has missed only one home game.

"I was with the UMD hockey team for a Friday-Saturday series against Michigan in Ann Arbor. We were due back in the Twin Cities at eight o'clock Sunday morning, and I had a Vikings game at one o'clock. I actually was wondering how to kill time before the game. I needn't have worried. An ice storm hit Detroit, and the airport closed down." Nothing got out, including Marsh.

Besides that one missed game, there have been some close calls.

"Another time, I was coming in from Denver with the

Bulldogs. It was an hour-40-minute flight to the Twin Cities which, with the time change, would give me an hour and 20 minutes to get to the Vikings game at Met Stadium. Plenty of time. I figured I'd have an hour before my first announcement.

"I was wrong. The flight was delayed in Denver because the incoming plane we were to use was late. Fortunately, the stewardess and the pilot were both Vikings fans and, when I explained my problem, they radioed ahead to the North Central Airlines terminal and they called Merrill Swanson at the Vikings public relations office to say I'd be late.

"A KDLH photographer met me at the airport when we got in at 12:15, but we got stuck in traffic, and I got to the Met at twenty minutes to one. Merrill had arranged for Tony Parker to stand by in case I didn't make it. As I walked into the booth, Tony was just about to make his first announcement. He looked up at me, breathed a sigh of relief and said, 'Boy, I'm sure glad to see you!' I looked at him and said, 'I'm glad to see you, too.' It was like a Greek chorus.

"Then there was the time I stayed overnight in south Minneapolis. My assistant, Joe Vatalaro, was to pick me up at 11:30 Sunday morning for a one o'clock Vikings game. 'JoJo,' who was usually dependable, never showed up. Finally, I called a cab and told the driver I had only 15 minutes to get to the Met. She drove down the median, across sidewalks, on the shoulder, in and out of traffic and got me to the stadium with 10 minutes to spare!"

Another auto trip ended painfully one Saturday morning on Highway 23 a few miles south of Duluth.

"JoJo and I were heading to Morris to do a UMD-Minnesota-Morris football game on radio. We had a KDAL car, and I was driving. I'm still not sure what happened or why, but a car took a left turn in front of us without signaling, there was a crash and we were suddenly in the trees. Both of us ended up in St. Mary's hospital."

Marsh's right thumb was fractured. Vatalaro suffered several broken ribs. The car was totaled.

There have been some interesting trips by air, too.

"One was a flight with Kevin Pates of the *Duluth News-Tribune*, heading for a UMD hockey game in Colorado Springs. We got to Denver OK, but the connecting flight was canceled.

"The smart thing would have been to rent a car and split the cost between the newspaper and KDAL, but we saw a sign that said 'Bus to Colorado Springs,' and decided to be economical. We were still waiting in line when the bus filled up. It was three hours later before we finally got another bus.

"It turned out to be a local, a real milk run that stopped at every bus station in south Denver. Not only that, but the driver took back roads I doubt he could find again and stopped at every village, even up in the hills.

"I was looking at my watch. I had to get to the game early to do interviews and set up the equipment. By six o'clock, we were still somewhere around Castlerock.

"Fortunately, a couple of young women on the bus told us their boyfriends were meeting them in the Springs. We pulled into the depot about 6:30, an hour 'til game time. The bell captain stowed our gear while the women talked their young men into driving us to the Broadmoor. We got there at five to seven—26 minutes to hook up the gear and interview both coaches. The station announcer had been frantically trying to call me over the broadcast line for about an hour. Without those young women, we'd surely have been late—or missed the game entirely."

As any prudent Northlander knows, considering the winter weather must always be part of any travel plan. Winters in Minnesota's Arrowhead can be dangerously frigid—like one night when Marsh was master of ceremonies for a program on the Range. The occasion was a football banquet honoring Buhl, the season's Range champions. Murray Warmath, then head football coach at Minnesota, was main speaker, along with assistant Gopher coach Denver Crawford.

"By the time the ceremonies were over, the temperature outside was 25 below," Marsh recalls. "I had my own car, and Murray and Denver were traveling together in a university car, so we decided to leave at the same time and stay close, in case something went wrong in one car. I started out alone, with Warmath and Crawford about a mile behind me. I was almost to Duluth when I got stopped by a traffic light at the Highway 53 entrance to the air base. When I stopped, the engine quit. Of course, so did the heater. The car wouldn't restart.

"Until it happens, you don't realize how fast a car can cool off. Murray and Denver weren't more than a couple of minutes behind me but, in that short time, I nearly froze. Murray drove me to the old Highland Supper Club, and we must have asked everybody in there for jumper cables. Finally, we found some and got my car started. My first stop was at an all-night gas station for my own set of cables. I've carried them ever since."

There were never any guarantees, even when traveling with the teams.

"One of our bus rides from Madison in the early days I'll never forget. It was 18 or 20 below, and the bus heating system failed a few miles outside Madison. That bus got cold quick. All the guys dug into suitcases and equipment bags for extra clothing— sweaty socks, sweaty uniforms, old towels—anything to wrap up in. By the time we got to Duluth, it was 25 below outside and almost that cold in the bus."

One terrifying incident nearly cost Marsh and his traveling companions their lives.

"Erv Goldfine [Duluth businessman and former University of Minnesota regent] owned a piece of the Green Bay Packers at that time. In the past, I'd helped host bingo games and serve breakfast on the Goldfines' football trains from Duluth to the

Twin Cities and, this particular day, Erv invited me to fly to a Packers-Cowboys game in Green Bay with him and his two young sons, John and Steve. He'd rented a six-place Piper Cherokee and, when we took off from Duluth, it was about 20 below.

"That's the coldest football game on record: December 31, 1967. When we landed at Austin Straubel field, the wind was blowing so hard you couldn't catch your breath. We had choice seats—first row, 50-yard line—and we'd brought along a stack of old newspapers to sit on as insulation on the ice-cold concrete stands in Lambeau Field. I made the mistake of taking my mittens off at halftime to hold a cup of coffee. My fingers were cold through the whole second half.

"I didn't think there was a chance they'd play football in weather like that, but they did. The Packers won on that famous quarterback sneak by Bart Starr with seconds left to play.

"Unfortunately, we neglected to reserve a starting motor for the plane. When we got back to the airport, there were nearly a hundred private planes trying to get started. We waited our turn in the lounge, rehashed the game, and I had a chance to talk to some of the Dallas players. I thought Don Meredith was a very personable guy for a player who'd just lost a crucial heartbreaker. It turned out that Dandy Don and the rest of the Cowboys were back in Dallas on their chartered jet before we ever left Green Bay.

"When we finally did get into the air it was dark and, after replaying the game again, we went on to other subjects—like what would happen in case of an emergency out there in the night. Our pilots, a couple of UMD students named Terry Johnson and Bill Budris, explained that they'd look for city lights or a large open spot like a lake for an emergency landing."

Barely 10 minutes later the engine sputtered and died—the *only* engine.

"Let me tell you, that's the loneliest feeling in the world: 6,000 feet up, 20 below outside and sudden silence. To be honest, I never thought we'd make it. I fully expected some northern Wisconsin pine tree to come through the windshield at any moment.

"The windshield and side windows were icing up, and we held our hands against the inside of the Plexiglas to melt a space big enough to see. The co-pilot was on the radio calling 'May Day,' and Terry was trying to restart the engine, looking around for a spot to light and all the time, we were losing altitude.

"Suddenly, through that ice-covered windshield, somebody spotted the lights of a car below. We found out later it was a man and his wife on their way to a New Year's Eve party at a nearby road house. When we were about 200 feet up, Terry flicked on the landing lights, and we were able to pick out Highway 118, a few miles south of Ashland.

"It was snow-covered, but he put the plane down so smoothly that all we did was tip over a farmer's mailbox with a wing. I've had rougher landings on commercial jets, under more choice conditions than we had that cold night on a rural highway. It was a beautiful job of flying. Terry later went on to become a pilot for Republic Airlines.

"By the time we stepped out of the plane, the car we'd spotted from the air had turned around and was back. Erv was white as a sheet, as I was, but he's a trouper. He told the driver and his wife, 'We're shooting a TV commercial!' I said, 'Yeah, for a Goldfine's plane crash sale!'

"Within a few minutes, there were a half-dozen cars there, including the Wisconsin Highway Patrol, sheriff's deputies and police. We found out a North Central Airlines flight had picked up our May Day and followed us, radioing our position to the authorities."

The night's misfortune didn't end there. The group rented a car in Ashland for the drive back to Duluth. On the way, the car skidded off an icy highway and came to rest in a snowbank. No one was hurt.

"It was my most memorable New Year's Eve," Marsh says with a wry smile. "If there's such a thing as having nine lives, like a cat, I probably used up a couple of mine that night."

# CHAPTER NINE

# The Tug of Home

H e wasn't home much when we were growing up. But the times when we were all together were very special."

Ginger Nelson looks across the table at her dad and smiles. Her auburn hair catches the sun streaming through the windows of the revolving skytop restaurant atop the Radisson Hotel. Her eyes, brown like her father's, sparkle as she glances out at the Duluth harbor and the Aerial Lift Bridge that is the city's unique trademark.

"We'd see a lot of my dad during the summer, but from October 'til April he traveled with the hockey team. Many times, on weekend road trips, he'd get back to the Twin Cities on Sunday and rush right to a Vikings game. We hardly saw him during the hockey season unless we'd go to the home games."

Ginger, oldest of three children by Marsh's previous marriage, lives in San Francisco's Bay Area where she's a telecommunications specialist.

Greg, who occasionally assists Marsh with television sports coverage on Channel 3, and Nancy, the youngest, both live in

Duluth. They all learned early to adjust their home life to the demands of their father's radio and television schedule.

"He always worked holidays when everybody else had a day off," Ginger says. "I remember him coming in at the last minute on Christmas Eve, and then everything was wonderful. He doesn't like to party on New Year's Eve, so he'd volunteer to work so somebody else at the station could have the night off.

"I don't recall ever being disciplined by my dad. I just remember that he wasn't home very much but, when he was home, he dished out love. He'd hug us and play with us. He'd put us on his shoulders and stomp around the house to his collection of march records."

Things happened fast for the Nelsons, even the family vacations. In a burst of enthusiasm, Marsh planned them on the spur of the moment.

"He came home for dinner one evening and announced that we were going to Washington, D. C., on vacation. We had two days to get ready," Ginger recalls. "Everything was on a deadline. We had fun in Washington, but he rushed us through the Smithsonian Institution in about four hours so he could take us down into Virginia and show us where he was stationed in the Army. I'd rather have spent more time at the Smithsonian, or Ford's Theater.

"Planning was always a little loose," she recalls. "One time, when we were little kids, we lost Greg on Mackinac Island. We were all riding bikes along the trails and Greg just wandered off. Dad was worried but tried not to show it. He had the authorities out combing the woods for Greg, but he finally just showed up on his own, pedaling down the main street."

Time was always the enemy. Only on fishing trips did they not race the clock. Marsh shared this cherished pastime often with all three children.

"I fished with Dad a lot. I didn't always want to, but I didn't always have a choice," Ginger says with a roll of her eyes. "We'd sit in the boat for hours and nothing would happen. We'd bring books along and even sleep. We were bored senseless."

On one dismal morning Marsh, his father, and Ginger climbed into the boat in a chilling rain and headed out across the lake. "I was about seven years old," she says. "It was a miserable day and I thought it was the worst thing he and Grandpa could put me through. But, all of a sudden, there were fish! We couldn't haul them in fast enough. The boat was full in about an hour."

Marsh grins and pats her shoulder.

"You kids never believed my stories about the great fishing in Lake Vermilion when I was young," he says, "and I don't think I ever saw you so happy and enthusiastic as that day you found out there really were fish in there."

"He's very persuasive," Judy says. "Shortly after we met, he told me one day, as he was about to rush off somewhere, 'I'm selfish and I usually get what I want. Someday I'm going to marry you, whether you like it or not! Wait for me!' I didn't know whether he meant I should wait right there, or wait until he got around to it."

He got around to it, but in his own sweet time.

"He squeezed me in between hockey broadcasts, literally," Judy says. "He said, 'I have one free weekend in October. After that, I don't get a weekend off until April.'"

On the day before Halloween they went grouse hunting. That evening, with only family members and a few close friends in attendance, Judith Lovold and Marsh Nelson were married in Judy's home town, Knife River, on Lake Superior's North Shore.

"The following weekend, he was in New York," Judy recalls with a wry smile. "Ever since, it's been rush, rush, from one thing to another, in everything we do, everywhere we go."

Marsh shrugs. "Honey, it's the nature of the job."

There was one day when the press box got an unexpected treat.

"I wanted to do something special for Marsh's 59th birthday," Judy says, "and I wanted it to be a total surprise. September 13 was on a Sunday in 1988; so, of course, Marsh was doing the Vikings' stadium announcing at the Dome."

Judy picked up the phone and called Kernal Buhler of the Vikings public relations staff and asked if she could bring a birthday cake up to the press box for the national and local media.

"Absolutely!" Buhler said. Judy reminded him that Marsh had been the Vikings' stadium voice for a quarter century and suggested an appropriate greeting on the Metrodome's electronic scoreboard. "I'll take care of it," he promised.

Marsh had no idea that the cake rode with them to Minneapolis in the trunk of the car. "It was the largest sheet cake the Patty Cake Shop [in Duluth] makes."

The cake was a halftime hit in the press box, but the real surprise for Marsh was when he glanced up at the scoreboard and read: "Happy 59th Birthday to Marsh Nelson, our stadium announcer."

"The Viking band played 'Happy Birthday' and the whole stadium crowd sang," Judy recalls.

Later, Harvey Solon couldn't believe it.

"You set that up?" he asked Judy. "That took real guts!"

People ask Marsh why he's stayed in Duluth. Surely, the argument goes, there were opportunities to move to lucrative broadcast jobs where fame is wider, audiences are bigger and pay is fatter.

"I guess I've stayed because it's home. I'm two hours from Tower, my mother lived there until she moved into a Duluth nursing home in 1988. I love the country and the people," he says.

"Then, too, I don't like the intensity of big city markets—five o'clock traffic snarls, the dog-eat-dog rivalry of the stations and the frantic pace. At KSTP, I was No. 3 in the sports department, right after Nesbitt and Tighe, but I felt more pressure and competition there, as the third man, than I did when I came to Duluth as sports director. Here, the pace is a little slower by comparison. There's something to be said for being a big fish in a smaller pond."

He's had opportunities to leave KDAL and Channel 3.

"Odin [Ramsland] told me many times: 'I can get you on at WGN any time you're ready,' but I was never ready to live and work in Chicago. I love Duluth.

"One of the toughest things was saying no to my friend Paul Giel. Paul was at the University of Minnesota when I was at Macalester, and I'd watch him play football and baseball. We'd go over to Delta Field—Bierman Field now—and you could always tell when Paul was pitching, without asking or reading the papers. If there were 1,500 people on hand, and 10 or 15 major league scouts in the stands, you knew Giel was on the mound. If there were maybe 200 people there, and no scouts, Giel wasn't pitching that day. He went on to play pro with the Giants and the Twins. He was truly a great athlete."

Giel was sports director at WCCO in Minneapolis in the 1960s when he approached Marsh. Larry Jagoe, who produced Minnesota Twins games on radio, had just announced his resignation to join a Minneapolis advertising agency, creating a rare job opening at the station.

"Paul came to Duluth and tried to hire me. I met with him and, later on, with 'CCO's general manager at the Minneapolis airport. I thought about it carefully. At the time, 'CCO was doing North Star hockey and I'd be working with Al Shaver, which would be fun. But I wouldn't be doing any television. 'CCO radio and TV are entirely separate operations.

"As for producing Twins games, I thought about all those nice summer days when I could be out in a boat fishing, instead of at Met Stadium worrying about whether Halsey Hall and Herb Carneal had remembered to pick up their commercials, and having to tell those veterans when to talk and when not to.

He smiles and shrugs an open-hand gesture of helplessness.

"So I said no. How the hell did I know that a few months later Paul Giel would leave to become athletic director at the university? I'm not saying I'd have filled his radio job at the station, but I'd certainly have been on the spot as a contender."

Marsh admits to wanting only one other job: sports information director at the U.S. Air Force Academy at Colorado Springs. Military protocol beat him out.

"My friend Bernie Raetz, who was on the coaching staff, had been at St. Thomas College when I was at Macalester, and he introduced me to Ben Martin, the academy's head football coach. I guess I impressed Martin because Bernie told me later, 'Ben really wants you for the information job.'

"But Air Force brass thought the academy should have a serviceman as SID. Ben Martin didn't agree. He said, 'I don't want an Air Force man. We play a lot of civilian schools, too.' Nevertheless, they assigned a uniformed man."

Other chances came and went.

"Ralph Romano [former Bulldog hockey coach] became acting athletic director at UMD when Lloyd Peterson got to the end of his reign and retired. Then, when Ralph passed away, the job opened up again. As a state institution, UMD had to advertise, and they got a lot of applications. Some of my friends threw my name in the hat, but I never really tried for it."

He grows serious as he sips a steaming mug of coffee and bites into one of Judy's fudge brownies. He brushes a crumb from his purple sweater bearing the Minnesota Vikings staff emblem.

"I never had a job I didn't like but, in this business, you sacrifice a lot of yourself, and so do the people close to you. You learn to live with the clock, and it becomes a way of life."

Marsh loves what he does but, with close friends, particularly those who share and have shared broadcast experience, he'll admit to some frustrations.

"I don't think I've improved or grown a bit in the 39 years I've been on the air. Maybe it's simply that I don't have any more ability, but the tight show we have limits sports to little more than the basics—and that we have to rush.

"For many years, our two condensed half hours of news-weather-sports, at 6 and 10, shrank even more when they stuffed promos into the segments—30-second 'give-aways.' I'd come in some nights and the news anchor would say, 'Guess what, Marsh. I've got nine minutes of news time.' Nine minutes of news in a 30-minute program block!

"I'm supposed to have five minutes for sports, not counting the commercials, but I used to come at the end of the half-hour segment, so I'm the buffer. If everybody else runs over, or there's a lot of extra chatter between the news anchors and the weather forecaster, it all comes together at my end of the show. Some nights, I'd be down to two or three minutes. How can you properly cover sports like that? But, lately, it's been a little better.

"You learn to live with not having enough time, enough equipment, enough people—even enough cameras, tape editors or station cars. We're not alone. It's the same with most stations in small and medium-size markets. The key to surviving is cramming as many commercial spot announcements as possible into every time slot. You do your best with what's left, and you find satisfaction in knowing you've done just that.

"Years ago I advised my son, Greg—and a lot of other youngsters who ask me about getting into radio and television—to forget about sports announcing as a career. It's just too hard to crack these days. There aren't that many jobs available, and too many people are after the few there are. Sure, you can work for pennies in some country peanut-whistle but, unless you're very lucky with miracles, that's a dead end.

"When I came out of the Army, it was a little different. Then, back in the 1950s, new radio stations were just coming on the air—more chances to break in on the ground floor. From there, it was even possible to go on to the big time—the networks. I've known several who did. Today, the networks only want the big name athletes, the superstars, for broadcast sports. I can understand that. A lot of money rides on TV sports. The networks can only make money by delivering a viewing audience to advertisers. Pat Summerall, O.J. Simpson, Merlin Olsen, Terry Bradshaw or John Madden will sell a lot more razor blades and Coke than Marsh Nelson or Jeff Papas."

From the outside, the career of a TV sports reporter looks deceptively simple and exciting but, as more than one novice has learned, from the inside it's a tough, demanding, unforgiving job.

"Ahmad Rashad, former Vikings wide receiver and one of my favorite people, is a good example," Marsh says with a smile. "He went from a regional station on to network television very successfully, but he's a rarity.

"Ahmad joined WCCO a few years ago while he was still with the Vikings. I'd see him from time to time and, shortly after he started, he said to me one day, 'Marsh, you guys in the media have the tough job: asking the right questions. You have to know a little bit about everything. My first assignment at 'CCO was to cover a high school tennis match. I didn't know anything about tennis and had no idea what to ask a tennis player. An athlete has it easy—just answer the questions you guys ask.'"

# CHAPTER TEN

# This Bud's for You

Rashad was right. Someone, probably an old journalism professor, declared that a good reporter can become an expert on any subject on a moment's notice. The professor exaggerated, of course, but not much.

Marsh Nelson's advice to broadcast-news hopefuls also is disarmingly simple: "Read, study, talk to people, and learn as much as possible *about* as much as possible . . . and remember it." Modestly, he neglects to mention native talent, a voice, diction, articulation, stage presence, the ability to read with authority—and a legion of true friends in both high and low places, personal and professional. It's a rare package. In nearly 40 years behind microphones and cameras, Marsh Nelson has wrapped it up quite nicely.

"In 27 years doing live hockey pickups for KDAL I met a lot of people who made a lasting impression on me. Some of them are no longer with us," Marsh says, idly toying with one of the hockey pucks on his desk. "On the road every weekend, you're the engineer, the play-by-play announcer, the interviewer, the guy who reads the commercials. It's strictly a one-man show and, if anything goes wrong, you fix it yourself, often with help from your competitors in the booth.

"I've shared grit and glory with those guys. When they came to Duluth and forgot a microphone or a piece of tape, we'd always help them out, and they did the same for me when I was on the road and needed something to get on the air—or stay on. It's a close, personal association. Nobody ever profited from a colleague's misfortune. It's not like that anymore. Now it's dog-eat-dog.

"At the top of my list is my long-time rival and close friend, the late Bob Junkert of WDSM. We had some interesting times together. Another was Bobby Olson at WMPL—'Whimple' in Hancock–who did Michigan Tech games for many years. And, at Grand Forks, Doug Tegmeier of KNOX was so highly regarded that, when he died a number of years ago, the state named the press box at the University of North Dakota after him.

"At some colleges, students were the hockey broadcasters. Ted Robinson, who's familiar to Twins and North Stars fans, started as a student announcer at Notre Dame's campus radio station. Every time I see him, he remembers the few words of encouragement and suggestions I gave him back in his student days.

"I also had great respect for the late Bob Martin, voice of the Denver University Pioneers and the Denver Broncos. We'd get together whenever the Bulldogs played Denver U and every two or three years when the Broncos and the Vikings played here. He got a special page, in his memory, in the 1990 Denver Bronco media guide—and he richly deserved it.

"I have a feeling of sadness when I talk about Tegmeier, Junkert and Martin. They were friends of mine over the years. Now, they've passed on."

He also singles out a few special favorites.

"My idol among hockey broadcasters is the late Dan Kelly of the St. Louis Blues who also did NHL broadcasts on network television. Probably second is our own North Stars' Al Shaver. They're both far and away the best, in my opinion.

"My all-time favorite baseball broadcaster is Chicago's Harry Caray. Although there never was any doubt about which team he was rooting for, he never shied away from giving the opposition an even shake—he always let you know when they turned in a good play, or if they weren't hustling. He called it the way it was.

"When a batter connected, you could tell by the tone of Harry's voice whether it was going to be a base hit or not. If his voice went up and he got excited, you could bet on the line drive. If he was matter-of-fact when the batter hit the ball, it usually turned out to be a fly somebody should have caught. Very few broadcasters have that knack."

Marsh doesn't hesitate to praise a couple of close friends.

"Locally, in Minnesota, Herb Carneal and Ray Christensen are both true professionals. They're genuine people, broadcasting and away from the microphone. I admire them both, for their loyalty and for the job they've done for sports over the years."

Along the way, Marsh also formed close ties with coaches, players and fans. Some were headliners, others just hard-working toilers in the trenches. He's no name dropper, and it takes a bit of coaxing, but in relaxed moments with friends he'll share some experiences and stories, as well as opinions gained first-hand, of the more colorful figures he's known on and off the air, particularly during his quarter-century as a staff member of the Minnesota Vikings.

Coaches come and coaches go, but Marsh puts his friend Bud Grant up front.

"He gave the Vikings class—like having his players line up straight at attention, helmets off, facing the flag for the national anthem. Now, most teams in the league do that.

"I think one thing that made Bud so successful as a football coach was the same thing that made Wayne Gretzky successful as a hockey player: they both were aware of everything going on around them at all times. I don't think Wayne's the greatest skater or the best shot in the world, but he's consistent—and he knows where every player is on the ice. Bud was like that as a coach. He was aware of everything and everybody on the field, every minute of the game. Nothing got by him.

"For instance, I remember one hot day at training camp in Mankato. It was scorching, about 100 degrees with humidity to match. The press corps wandered around trying to get out of the sun, and I found a spot in the shade of a blocking sled and stretched out on my back to watch. When practice was over, everybody wiped their brows and headed for the gate. Grant was walking alone, so I fell in alongside him and said something like, 'Boy, Coach, a tough one out there today.' He looked at me without smiling and said, 'It didn't look too tough out there where you were, Marsh.' Here's a guy with 100 players and 10 assistant coaches to watch on the field, and he noticed an insignificant reporter lounging in the shade. He never missed a thing.

"Bud was stern, disciplined, always in command, standing there on the sidelines like General Patton. I ran into that cold exterior one time. Whenever Bud and I got together, the talk was rarely about football. It usually centered around the local blueberry crop, fishing or hunting. One such time, late in the season, I happened to ask Grant what kind of a hunting season he'd had.

"'Great duck season!' he replied. 'Plenty of ducks just outside my place on the Minnesota River. How about you?'

"Well, I hesitated a minute and then admitted I hadn't bought a small game license in about a dozen years.

"Bud seemed stunned. He just looked at me with those icy blue-gray eyes and said, 'What! I've got some advice for you.' He was not really joking when he said, 'If you don't quit trying to broadcast all the games around Duluth and start enjoying life a little you're going to wind up in a cemetery—and there aren't any ducks in a cemetery!' Well, I got the same kind of feeling his quarterbacks must have experienced after throwing an interception. He wasn't happy to learn I hadn't done any hunting.

"He was universally fair, and one of his strongest characteristics was his loyalty. He never said or did anything that might give aid and comfort to the enemy. He never made a slurring remark about an opposing team, its coach or players—because he knew it would be in the press and posted in the visitor's locker room. He never chewed out a player in public or in front of teammates. Next to taking away a guy's one-game salary, that would be the worst thing he could do to a professional athlete. He had his heart-to-heart sessions with a player in private.

"Bud was respected rather than loved. A lot of people thought Ed Marinaro was a cocky Eastern playboy with a star complex, but Grant saw something else there. He and Ed respected each other. Bud told me a number of times, 'When Ed got here he was used to carrying the ball and didn't really know what blocking was all about. But, in time, he became very good at it.' He didn't mention his own role in changing Marinaro's attitude.

"The summer day Ed Marinaro showed up for training, he had shoulder-length hair. Next day, it was clipped short. Ed told me, 'I saw Tinglehoff and Bill Brown with short hair and The Man didn't have to tell me to cut mine.'"

Marsh's longtime friend, Duluth sports promoter Harvey Solon, once took on the unofficial job of trying to get Marsh a raise from the tight-fisted Vikings' front office.

"We were in the Viking locker room after a home game," Marsh recalls. "Harvey had played football with Grant at Minnesota back in the '40s, and was giving him a mild ribbing about my salary as the Vikings' stadium announcer. When Harvey paused for breath, Bud looked at him and said, 'Well, if you're his agent, you should get a cut.' Harvey snapped back, 'Yeah, for an agent around here, 15 percent of nothin' is still nothin.'"

Marsh smiles and flips through an old Vikings game book.

"Bud was sometimes blunt, especially with the Eastern writers who tried to ask deep, penetrating questions. For instance, somebody would ask him why he went for a field goal when the Vikings were on the enemy's five-yard line instead of trying for a first down and a touchdown drive. They expected some scientific, technical explanation of secret strategy. Bud wouldn't crack a smile. He'd simply say, 'I wanted three points.'"

Marsh shifts in his chair and tosses the book aside.

"Grant didn't let coaching dominate his life. He didn't often take a football game home with him like some other great coaches—Dick Vermeil, Bill Walsh, Vince Lombardi. Bud lived first, then coached.

"The Vikings were nearly always the last team to go to summer training camp. Bud would say it was because they were veterans and didn't need as much time to get ready. That's baloney, of course. He held off 'til the last minute because he wanted to spend as much time as possible with his wife Pat at his lake place near Gordon, Wisconsin, while some of his friends with the Bears, the Lions and the Packers were sweating it out in hundred-degree temperatures. His family took first priority.

"The Vikings had the perfect combination back in the 1970s: Bud Grant on the field and Jim Finks in the front office. It was no accident that they dominated the National Football Conference in those days. Bud was allowed to coach; Finks was allowed to run the front office.

"Finks is probably the most highly regarded executive in sports. It's not unusual for other general managers, when they run into front office problems, to call on Jim for help. For example, when Wellington Mara of the New York Giants, or the Steelers' Art Rooney would hit a snag, they wouldn't hesitate to ask Finks for advice.

"He had the universal respect and admiration of his peers. Recently, when Brian Burke took over in the National Hockey League as general manager of the Vancouver Canucks, he spent a week in New Orleans studying Finks' management style with the Saints, and he brought a lot of ideas back to Vancouver. That's a pretty good indication of how Jim Finks is regarded. It was a different game, but management principles are the same.

"He was always great to me. Each year, at the beginning of the football season, Finks would call me and say, 'When UMD's hockey schedule is set, I want you to save a weekend or two for a couple of trips with the Vikings.' I made several to the East and West Coasts, always a guest of the team and Jim Finks. I haven't taken a Vikings road trip since Jim left.

"I think it was a tragedy when Finks left the Vikings. It wouldn't have taken much to keep him here. All he wanted was a small piece of the action in a team he was building. If each of the five owners at the time had given him just one percent, he'd have been satisfied. Ole Haugsrud and Bernie Ridder were perfectly willing to do that, but it was a three-to-two vote. So, Finks went to the Chicago Bears, and also put in a couple of seasons as president of the Cubs, before he moved on to become president of the New Orleans Saints. Now the Saints are a major contender in the league, largely due to Jim Finks. He often told me the most enjoyable part of his career was the time spent in the Twin Cities."

In contrast to Finks was his successor as Vikings general manager, Mike Lynn.

"I didn't have much contact with Mike," Marsh says. "He'd walk through the press box and not say hello to anybody. I think he's a brilliant businessman, though—maybe too brilliant for the good of some of the players.

"The Vikings are noted for their tight purse strings. It's a small thing, I know, but it's traditional for the home team to provide free lunch and refreshments in the press box. Some teams lay out a real feast before the games: roast beef, steak, fish, with all the trimmings. Not the Vikings. The Vikings were noted for being frugal from the start.

"For instance, the North Stars, who play about 40 home games a season, put out a full meal, including salads. The Vikings, on the other hand, play maybe 10 games at home in a season, including a couple of exhibitions—they serve chili and hot dogs to the press. Polish sausage if we're lucky. The Vikings have always been a very successful team; never had to worry about sellouts, ticket buyouts or giveaways. Their TV contract is far superior to what baseball and hockey teams get, so it isn't a case of losing money on the chow. They could set a better table. It got a little better, though, under Mike Lynn."

Marsh grows serious for a moment.

"A general manager has to be a bit of a gambler, and Mike Lynn took some chances—and won. He went out on a limb to make a deal with the Giants for Gary Zimmerman and to get some of the players out of the U.S. Football League. He pulled a master stroke with Miami and beat out Detroit for Anthony Carter and probably got a lot of help in that deal from Bud Grant and Burnsie [Vikings Head Coach Jerry Burns]. But Mike mortgaged the future on the Herschel Walker trade. He knew what he wanted and went after it. Walker is a great player—but 12 men for a running back? Wow!"

Marsh pours another cup of coffee. "Players are players," he says, "but it's some sort of axiom that a team's only as good as the man at the top, especially in football, whether that man's in the front office or on the sidelines calling the shots. The successful franchises over the years—Dallas, the Raiders, Miami—have all had exceptional leadership, regardless of who the players were."

He cites Norm Van Brocklin, the Vikings' first coach, as one example of effective field leadership in difficult times.

"A lot of his magic was his football knowledge, his own record as a brilliant player. He was recognized as an absolute offensive genius. In the formative years, the Vikings got the castoffs from some other teams—a combination of veterans and rookies. Some had played on three, four or five teams before they landed with the newly formed Vikings.

"A lot of Van Brocklin's early success was due to personal charisma, his own record as a quarterback and his ability to inspire. His players respected him because many of them had played with him or against him. The rookies looked on him with awe because he'd just retired as an active player and had been a dominant quarterback at his peak."

It was a curious collection of football players that came together that first season at Bemidji.

"Everybody reacts differently to a coach. Norman had rules and regulations, and sometimes they were broken but never more than once if he knew about it. He was tough on the practice field, but I don't think he was as stern an individual as Bud Grant. Bud ruled by reputation.

"I've been going to the opening training camp ever since that first Vikings gathering under Van Brocklin in 1961. We'd heard about how he was a gruff, take-charge guy on the field. Apparently he was, but he also was very gracious with the media because he knew that, with a new franchise, he could use all the publicity he could get, anywhere—in small-town newspapers and television, on the networks or in metropolitan dailies."

From the very first, Marsh has been rubbing shoulders with the Vikings, from draft-choice rookies to the greats like Alan Page, Carl Eller, Jim Marshall, Gary Larsen and Doug Sutherland—the famed "Purple People Eaters."

Some players became notable for different reasons.

"I always had high regard for Tommy Kramer," Marsh says, "but, unfortunately, Tommy hit his peak at the wrong time: when the team was at its lowest ebb—not necessarily due to Kramer, but to the fact that the Vikings didn't have the material. There were some years when the only Viking in the Pro Bowl was a 42-year-old place kicker, Jan Stenerud. The talent was very meager, overall, for several seasons when Tommy was at his peak.

"Tommy has a great background and showed it all through his career. His dad was a coach, his brothers were athletes and he knows football backward and forward. He played at Rice, where they used a pro system on offense. He's a great competitor, despite some times, later in his career, when his performance was somewhat disappointing.

"It's unfortunate that Tommy didn't come on the scene six or seven years later when there was more talent around him, after the Vikings got some pretty good players from the old United States Football League. When Kramer was coming up as a rookie, I remember Grant telling me: 'This guy is about as well-equipped a quarterback as ever came into this league.' But, with the injuries he's sustained, plus a few off-field problems, things didn't work out as well as they should have.

"Personally, he's a little like Tarkenton, aloof from the press and the fans. But once you get him talking, he'll talk forever."

"Francis [Tarkenton] was unapproachable when he had something on his mind or was heading for a team meeting. But if you'd get him aside when he had time, he'd talk all day. He's very honest and direct. His father was a minister, and Fran is sincerely religious. That may have led to some of his problems with Van Brocklin—'Stormin' Norman.' The Dutchman used language that would fit right in on the waterfront docks. I think that sometimes rubbed Tarkenton the wrong way because of his religious upbringing."

Spicy language is the hallmark of the Vikings' current head coach, Jerry Burns.

"You can hear him all over the practice field. Bud Grant didn't say a lot. He'd just walk around and observe, with his hands folded across his chest. Burns makes up for Grant's silence.

"But the players genuinely like Burns. I think they respect a coach like Grant or Lombardi but, with Burns, it's 'like' as well as 'respect.' Everybody calls him 'Burnsie,' and that's a pretty good hint of real affection. And I think there was mutual respect between Grant and Burns during the years they were together, both at Winnipeg and the Vikings.

"He's very precise in everything, as head coach and through his years as the Vikings' offensive coordinator. He lets you know what he expects, in unmistakable terms and easy-to-understand language. When you run a play for Burns in practice, and the pattern says you run down nine yards and cut to your right, you go down *nine* yards—not eight, not ten. Burns will scream at the receivers in practice drills if they don't run the pattern exactly as it's supposed to be."

Ole Haugsrud, one of the five original Vikings owners, was one of Marsh's closest friends.

"I knew him for about 18 years, through our connection with the Vikings, and also while we were both active in the Fatherless Boys Association. He'd take great delight, around Christmas time, in bringing a couple of signed Vikings footballs, posters or some other team trinket to give away to the kids at the FBA Christmas party. It was hard to tell who was more excited, Ole or the kids.

"Ole was mainly responsible for getting the Vikings franchise for Minnesota, and some people credit him with saving the NFL when he signed the great Ernie Nevers to the old Duluth Eskimos back in the 1920s.

"I had a great time with Ole and his wife Margaret during our trip to the Scandinavian countries in 1965, the year the Twins were driving for the American League pennant. There's a statue of Winston Churchill in a Copenhagen courtyard, and Ole, who was in the cigar business, just happened to have a stogie with him. He climbed up to pose with the statue, and held that cigar to Winnie's mouth, 'compliments of Ole Haugsrud and the CCC Canteen.'

"Another time, in Göteborg, Sweden, we drove by the new Ulivi Stadium. The lighting system there was spectacular: only two light towers, but they were so high-intensity they lit the stadium, plus a lot of the surrounding area. Ole insisted we take a taxi over to see it.

"There was a soccer match going on when we got there, but Ole wasn't about to buy a ticket just to see the stadium. In a loud voice, he mentioned that I worked for the *Chicago Tribune*. It was true, in a way, I guess—KDAL was owned by the *Tribune* at the time. Anyway, the words '*Chicago Tribune*' worked like magic. They couldn't do enough for us. They ushered us into the press box, choice seats, brought us beer and sandwiches and made us right at home. Later, as we were walking out, Ole laughed and said, 'Wait 'til we tell Harvey Solon we crashed the gate at Ulivi Stadium!'"

Marsh shifts in his chair and studies his hands for a moment.

"One of the highest honors I ever received, and the saddest, was when the family asked me to do the eulogy at Ole's funeral. Afterward, Bud Grant came up to me and told me it was one of the finest tributes he'd ever heard."

A few of those words, spoken from the heart at the passing of a close friend, are worth repeating:

"We were all thrilled listening to him recall the glorious days of the Kelly-Duluths, the Eskimos, the legendary accomplishments of Johnny Blood, the Rooneys, Nevers, Stein, Carlson. How proud Ole was to talk of these gentlemen, how he used to delight in the early days of pro football, the heavy schedules, the small rosters. He'd add, with a sly wink, 'Sometimes, it looked like I'd have to play.'

". . . When we think of the void in our lives that the passing of Ole Haugsrud means . . . let's also rejoice that anyone who came into contact with Ole surely is richer and far better for having known him."

# CHAPTER ELEVEN

# Highlights and Insights

**M**arsh pours a mug of coffee from the pot that's never empty in the Nelson kitchen. This is one of those rare moments when he feels like talking about friends in sports, the great and near-great. "It's funny how a seemingly insignificant thing can mean a great deal to someone," he says. "Dan Devine is a case in point."

Devine, born and reared in Proctor, immediately south of Duluth, was head coach of the Green Bay Packers at the time, and the Pack had arrived at Met Stadium for a game with the Vikings.

"When I got there, one of the Packers' assistant coaches was sitting at my place in the press box," Marsh remembers. "He said, 'Coach Devine would like to see you before the game.' I knew Dan, of course, but I was surprised. This was highly unusual. Coaches and players never talk to the media before a game, much less the stadium announcer, unless it's something special. I was still wondering when I walked into the Packer dressing room and Dan took me aside.

"'Marsh,' he said, 'I'd like to ask a favor.'"

I knew that his wife, Joanne, had been ill for a long time. Dan asked if I could get a greeting put on the electronic scoreboard for her, that it would help cheer her up. I said 'sure' and talked to my boss, Merrill Swanson. Within minutes, the sign lit up with 'Welcome Joanne Devine and the Green Bay Packers.' After the game, Dan couldn't thank me enough for that small favor.

"Dan Devine is one of my favorite people, and there have been some others through the years. Some I've had the privilege of knowing better than others, but I've salted away some great memories, and I treasure the friends and associations I've been fortunate enough to have in this business.

"Take Joe Namath, for instance." Marsh smiles and is silent for a moment. "I sure got a lesson in the fallacy of snap judgments.

"I first met Namath while he was still with the New York Jets, when they came to town to play the Vikings in Metropolitan Stadium. I suppose I was like most people: I thought he was a wise guy, a *prima donna* playboy. After all, you don't get a name like 'Broadway Joe' by staying home playing chess by the fire.

"Coach Weeb Ewbank had left orders that none of his players could grant interviews. After the game, photographer Adam Jaros and I ran into Ewbank outside the Jets dressing room, and I asked him for a couple of comments on tape. He said, 'Sure. Wait here. I'm meeting some friends at the main gate, but I'll be back in a minute.'

"As he walked away, Jaros and I had the same idea. The crowd had thinned out, nobody was around, and most of the team was already gone. We just opened the door and slid into the locker room. Namath was just coming out of the shower with a towel wrapped around him. I asked him if he'd talk to us and he said, 'Absolutely. Sit down.' He was a perfect gentleman, one of the most polite, down-to-earth people I've ever met.

"We talked while he toweled off and dressed. Before he put on his pants, he sat down on the bench and strapped on a couple of heavy metal knee braces. A lot of athletes wear knee braces—when they play. Namath's knees were so bad he had to wear those things just to walk out to the bus. I was deeply impressed by his courtesy and humility, but more especially by his courage. At that moment, my respect for Joe Namath went up 100 percent. And, it stayed there. I became a fan for life.

"Bobby Hull's another in the same mold. We used to see Bobby several times when he came to Duluth to watch his son Brett play for UMD. He's one of the most gracious sports people I've come in contact with. He's a tremendous interview.

"I remember one time when the Blackhawks played an exhibition game in the Duluth Arena. The incident's typical of Bobby Hull. He didn't go to the dressing room between periods like the other players. He stayed there in the runway, talking to kids and signing autographs. And, when the game was over, he was one of the last people out of the arena. He told me, 'As long as there's someone here who wants an autograph, I'll stay. These people pay my salary.'"

Marsh recalls an incident typical of Hull's attitude.

"Through KDLH's connection with WGN, we got special permission from Rudy Pilous, the Blackhawk coach, to do a pre-game interview with Bobby and co-star Stan Mikita. A taxi was waiting at the door to take them to the arena, and the driver was getting very impatient. Bobby smiled and pointed at me. He said, gently: 'Driver, whenever this man is finished we'll get in the cab.'

"Media here are different from the east coast and west coast writers," Marsh says. "I think the treatment Ted Williams used to get is a good example. In the big markets, the writers would cut Ted to pieces just for the sake of a column or a story to sell papers.

"Williams would come to Ely nearly every fall to hunt deer, and he has a lot of friends there. George Marsnik's sister worked at Vertin's Cafe in Ely, and one day she told George that Ted Williams was coming in for dinner. George and I were great fans when we were playing baseball for the BluSox, so we went over there just to catch a glimpse of Ted. He asked us to sit down and talk. We visited for an hour and a half about baseball, hunting and fishing. He was just like a guy off the street. 'Terrible Ted,' no. Great guy, yes."

In his office just off the KDLH-TV newsroom, Marsh reaches for a hockey puck from the stack on his cluttered desk.

"Among hockey coaches, there's no doubt John Mariucci was near the top. Just knowing 'Maroosh,' and playing for him when he was coaching the '56 Olympic squad, was a great experience.

"I first heard of Mariucci when he was playing football for Bernie Bierman around 1938, the golden era for the Golden Gophers. When he went into pro hockey with the Chicago Blackhawks, they called him 'Policeman on Ice,' or 'The Protector,' and for good reason. The Hawks had a great line—Doug and Max Bentley with Bill Mosienko—but they weren't big enough to take care of themselves in the rough- and-tumble NHL of those days. Mariucci was. He watched over them.

"Stories about Mariucci are endless. Another Olympic coach, my good friend Herb Brooks, played for him at Minnesota and recalls that Mariucci's practice sessions were as tough as regular games. One day, the Gophers were particularly sloppy—passes missed, skaters out of position—and Maroosh blew a blast on his whistle. Everything stopped and he roared: 'The more you guys practice, the worse you get. You get worse every day. The way you're playing today, you must think it's tomorrow!'"

Marsh chuckles and stands the trophy puck on edge.

"Mariucci had his own style and his own ideas about the game from his years with the Blackhawks. He bent the rules a little—or at least the spirit of the rules—when he was coaching at Minnesota.

"As an Eveleth boy, John learned a lot from coach Cliff Thompson, who probably produced more American-born hockey players than any single individual before or since. Cliff had many fabulous teams—kids he'd brought up from grade school. In the Depression years if a kid didn't have skates it wasn't unusual for Thompson to buy them with his own money.

"It happened that two of Thompson's former Golden Bears, Neal Celley and Johnny Matchefts, were part of Michigan's precision passing team, so Maroosh knew what he was up against when his Gophers played the Wolverines. He needed an edge. He got it, but in his own way, one night at a home game against Michigan in Minnesota's Williams Arena."

Marsh pauses for a moment, rolling the puck back and forth across the desktop.

"In order to pass properly, a puck has to lie flat on the ice." He flips the puck over and it wobbles to a stop, flat on the desk. "To cut down the bounce, game pucks are frozen and kept in a cooler until they're needed. The timekeeper brings them out in an ice bucket, right from the freezer.

"For this particular game, my Macalester coach, Hank Frantzen, was referee. Hank told me later, 'No kidding, Marsh, I stuck my hand in that bucket for a puck and there was warm water in there! Mariucci's hot pucks bobbled all over the ice! It raised hell with Michigan's passing game!'"

Putting the heat on opponents was a trick another Big Ten coach used to advantage. Michigan State's Amo Bessone's strategy was a little different. Marsh recalls one UMD-Michigan State game in East Lansing's Demonstration Hall:

"It seemed unusually warm in the arena, so I took off my jacket and rolled up my sleeves. When that didn't help, I walked down to the first row of seats to check the rinkside thermometer. I couldn't believe it! Eighty-two degrees! I found out later it was a Bessone gimmick. The Bulldogs were accustomed to cooler temperatures and Bessone had cranked up the heat to slow down their attack.

"He also had a tendency to be blunt. Some years ago, the Spartans were due to play the Russians in a tournament in Colorado Springs. Bessone called practice the night before. When they hit the ice, one of the guys yelled, 'Hey, Coach! Where's the pucks?' Bessone said, 'You'll practice without pucks tonight so you get used to it. Tomorrow, when you play the Soviets, you may not see the puck.'"

Marsh has special fondness for former UMD hockey coach Bill Selman, another stickler for discipline.

"His practice sessions were superbly controlled with military precision. When he blew his whistle everything stopped. If a player was halfway through a slap shot, that whistle stopped the shot in mid-swing. The puck just laid there. There wasn't even a follow-through."

Marsh chuckles as he leans forward to tell a story.

That first year at UMD (1968-'69) wasn't any bellringer for Selman. Marsh remembers, "He told me the only way to solve most of this team's problems was graduation. Then he went out and got good people: the likes of Cathedral's Pokey Trachsel, Chuck Ness, Lyn Ellingson of Duluth Central, Dave Roy and Allan Young from eastern Canada, Mike Stevens from Winnipeg, a complete line from Saskatchewan—Walt Ledingham, Murray Keogan and Cam Fryer. Selman built the best recruiting system the school ever had.

"The sad part of the story was that if he'd stayed, he'd have added to that great freshman class he brought in—people like Bobby Lawson, one of the greatest high school defensemen to come out of Minnesota. He followed Selman to St. Louis when he went there after Duluth.

"He recruited Larry Wright, the most sought-after junior player in western Canada. UMD had him for one year.

"One Saturday night in Colorado Springs—I've never seen

anything like it in 30 years of broadcasting hockey—Larry had two goals and hit the pipe twice, all in 45 or 50 seconds, on one line shift.

"When Selman left, Wright left. Bill told me, 'If I'd stayed, I'd have gone to Winnipeg and babysat him all summer to get him back.'

"That Colorado trip was the first hint of something wrong," Marsh recalls.

"When we got back, Sid Hartman had a little article in the *Minneapolis Tribune* saying that Coach Bill Selman wouldn't be returning to UMD next season. It was a bombshell to all of us. That was in February. Bill said he'd been told the previous October that his contract wouldn't be renewed. He told me, 'I didn't want to go public and tell you or Radar [Marsh's color broadcaster, Mike Radakovich] because I knew you guys'd churn up a storm. I thought if I just went along, kept quiet and turned out a good team they'd change their minds and bring me back.'

"He had a good record, something like 14 wins and eight losses, when the news broke. After the word got out, the 'Dogs lost their last seven games. Bill's discipline was gone when his lock on the players was broken, and they didn't play as well down the stretch.

"I'm convinced that had he not been let out after only two years, there'd have been NCAA championships right here in Duluth. Sports people all over the country recognized how lucky Duluth was to have him. A good example was that three-overtime loss to the Gophers in the Duluth Arena in 1970. The officials were a little late getting to the blue line and the Gophers definitely were offside. They scored a tying goal with about a minute to go, and won it in the third overtime with a goal by Mike Antonovich. That tally may have kept UMD out of the NCAA tournament. Later that night, I overheard an assistant coach from Cornell— the top team in the East at the time. He was telling somebody,

'I'm sure glad Duluth got beat because that's the best college hockey team in America.'"

Marsh stands the puck on edge again and gives it a push. It rolls off the desk and bounces across the floor into a corner. He does not retrieve it. Marsh was then, and still is, outspoken in his defense of Selman. Marsh and a coterie of cronies discussed what might be done to save the coach's job.

"About eight of us would meet regularly, several times a week. It was in the spring, and time was running out. Duluth attorney Al Weinberg pressed for a hearing. Selman thought about it a couple days and said no. 'I don't want to stir up a hornet's nest.' He already had the job at St. Louis.

"I think some people at the university thought they had a commitment from John MacInnis of Michigan Tech to come here. John was close to coming, too. During that final weekend, I talked to countless Tech alumni and, when Tech played here, those people weren't even watching the game. They were making phone calls to friends and alumni, trying to raise the ante to keep MacInnis at Houghton. Finally, they did sweeten the pot enough, and John stayed at Tech.

"So, MacInnis was out, Selman was gone and UMD didn't have a coach. They finally elevated assistant coach Terry Shercliffe to the job.

"There's no doubt in my mind that, given another year under Selman, UMD would have dominated the WCHA the way Wisconsin and Minnesota did for awhile. He was planning to build with Range kids and Duluth kids, plus the Canadians. Not to take anything away from Shercliffe and the others who followed, but when they let Selman go, it set UMD hockey back many years. Bill went on to St. Louis and did a fine job there until the school abandoned hockey. Then, he had fabulous success at Lake Superior State, turning a bunch of sometime toughs into a team of real gentlemen who distinguished themselves by their conduct.

"I think Mike Sertich has developed into fully as fine a coach as Selman. At the same time, I think Mike would agree that he learned a lot from Bill and absorbed a lot of the Selman philosophy when he played under him.

"One clue to Mike's success is his willingness to learn from others—Selman, Gus Hendrickson, Herb Brooks—and apply the best of what he's learned. He's very perceptive and gets something out of every game he watches. He can sit down with anybody—Bill Cleary of Harvard or Len Ceglarski of Boston College, for instance—and learn things from just a conversation.

"Just as important, he's surrounded himself with excellent assistants like Glenn Kulyk and Jim Knapp. A number of NHL scouts have told me they consider UMD's coaching staff the best in college hockey. I'd never argue that.

"He gets the best out of his players. Some kids who came through UMD with the Bulldogs wouldn't have done nearly as well playing for another team. Mike is able to talk to a kid, man to man, and make things happen with that young man. I don't think he knows any more hockey than the coach at the other end of the bench, but he's learned to apply what he does know. There's a purpose to everything Mike's players do on the ice.

"He's got a truly great philosophy of life. Mike's had some personal problems along the way, but he's overcome them, uses them as strength and shares them with others who are struggling. He's a complete person.

"Duluth is lucky Mike Sertich is still here. I think he was very close to going to Minnesota—and probably would have if he hadn't been high-pressured."

Marsh picks up a pencil stub and doodles on the calendar pad on his desk. "In my conversations with Mike, just two days before his final decision [in the spring of 1985], I was sure he was going. Later, I told Paul Giel [then University of Minnesota athletic director]: 'Paul, if it had been just you and Mike, Sertich would be your hockey coach.' But Mike's a small-town guy from Virginia and absolutely rebels against high-pressure salesmanship, the kind he got from some university alumni and sports boosters. I think he was spooked."

Marsh shakes his head. "I've heard it said that Sertich turned the job down because there'd be more pressure at Minnesota. That's ridiculous. The pressure's here. Hockey's the No. 1 sport in Duluth. You win or lose here, and everybody knows it. You win or lose at Minnesota, well, college hockey's about sixth in the priorities there, somewhere behind the Vikings, Twins, North Stars, Timberwolves and Gopher football and basketball. There wouldn't have been nearly the pressure there. When Mike turned down the Gopher job, they hired Doug Woog—and he's done a super job."

Marsh shifts in his chair and runs his fingers through his hair.

"As a matter of fact," he says, "UMD has been unbelievably fortunate with coaches. Very few men in college ball have had the brilliant career that Jim Malosky's had, a guy who played right alongside Bud Grant, Clayton Tonnemaker, Leo Nomellini and Billy Bye at Minnesota. Jim easily could have been head football coach at a big university. He has a fine grasp of fundamentals, as well as the game itself, and his practice sessions are as well organized as any in the business, including the pros.

"Just down the hall, Dale Race could certainly coach basketball at any school in the land. We're fortunate he likes the NAIA and Duluth.

"In Superior—or anywhere—the late 'Mertz' Mortorelli was a standout. During his years at UW-Superior, as a student, player and coach, he did as much for sports and athletes as anyone at any level. It's no wonder he's in nine halls of fame.

"Americo Mortorelli was one of the nicest guys you'd ever meet. He was the first athlete from UWS to sign a pro football contract, with the New York Giants in 1948. When he came back to UWS, he developed the athletic program from just two sports in 1954 to 11 in 1980, including his outstanding wrestling teams. For years, he and his wife Betty *were* the athletic program. I never met anyone who didn't like Mertz, and I don't think I ever knew a man who was more loyal to the philosophy that good, clean athletics brings out the very best in young people.

"He started mini leagues for area youth and helped develop coaching talent by sponsoring the Original Coaches Clinic of America for 17 years. They brought in such talent as Vince Lombardi, Ara Parseghian, Adolph Rupp, Al McGuire and other veterans to share their expertise with developing coaches. You could write a book about Mertz, and somebody should.

"I consider it a great honor, although a sad one, that of Mertz's six pallbearers, I was the only one who hadn't played football or wrestled for him."

Two other college coaches, Hall of Famer Herb Brooks of Minnesota and Wisconsin's Bob Johnson, rank high in Marsh's esteem.

"They were keen rivals in the 1970s," he says. "Herbie certainly was the reason behind the so-called 'Miracle on Ice' of the 1980 Olympics. His persistence and dedication had that 20-man squad all thinking his way by the time they hit the ice at Lake Placid.

"Herb was never too proud to ask for help. I recall, in December [1979] during the team's 60-game domestic tour, the Olympic team played UMD at Hibbing. Herbie asked me to ask Bulldog coach Gus Hendrickson if he could visit with him after the game—in private. He was concerned about how to handle Mark Pavelich. Gus had just coached Pav for several years at UMD, and Herbie wanted his advice on how to get the most out of this very talented player on the Olympic squad. Mark didn't always concentrate as much as he should have in practice sessions.

"Gus gave him the benefit of his experience, and Herbie used it to great effect. Later, he took Pav to the New York Rangers with him.

"Bob Johnson used to irritate some people who thought he had the idea that he invented hockey in Wisconsin. My feeling is that he deserved every accolade he received. He did a tremendous job with the Badgers.

"I recall the 1981 NCAA finals in Duluth. The Gophers and Badgers were due to meet in the arena for the college hockey title. Minnesota was a definite favorite. I went down to the arena about noon to do a pre-game interview with Johnson, and he told me, off the record, how he planned to win. 'Marsh,' he said, 'we're going to dump the puck down the ice, behind the Gopher net, every chance we get. I want their defensemen to handle the puck, not the Brotens and Bjugstad [Forwards Neal and Aaron Broten and Scott Bjugstad].' He knew what he was doing, and his strategy worked. Wisconsin beat Minnesota 6-3 for the title— doing just what Johnson said they'd do."

Recruiting potential powerhouse players is a vital part of a coach's job, a combination of salesmanship, diplomacy and luck. Marsh recalls a recruiting trip he made with the late UMD hockey coach, Ralph Romano.

"It was some years ago," he says. "Ralph had contacted Peter Fichuk of International Falls, Bruce McLeod of Fort Frances and Dave Merhar of Ely and asked me to go along with him one Saturday.

"We spent an hour or so with Fichuk in a Falls restaurant. Later, Ralph said, 'He was the hardest young man I've ever tried to recruit. We just couldn't pin him down!' Eventually, Minnesota's gain was UMD's loss.

"Across the border it was a different story. We met with Bruce McLeod, who was eager to come to Duluth. All Ralph wanted was a verbal commitment, but I think Bruce would have signed that very day. He did come to UMD, played on the line with Huffer Christiansen and Pat Francisco and stayed on to become UMD's athletic director.

"We drove on to my home town, Tower, stopped to see my

parents and then went on to Ely to visit Merhar. Dave was probably the single best high school hockey player in the state in the mid 1960s, but he leaned toward Minnesota. So Ralph asked me to take him on as a project.

"That spring, I watched four Stanley Cup hockey games on TV in the Merhar living room and talked a lot of hockey with Dave. It didn't do any good. We didn't get him in Duluth. He finally picked the U.S. Military Academy at West Point. He told me, 'I've heard it's very hard to get through the Point and I want to find out what kind of man I am.'

"He played very well for the Army's Division I hockey team and had a fine career in the Army. Last time I heard, it was Captain Merhar, one of the finest young men I ever knew, in or out of sports, in or out of the Army."

Not all of Marsh's favorites labored at the college level. A few high school mentors stand out, too.

"Marv Crowley at Superior and John Vucinovich at Duluth Central would have to be high on the list. They both had one thing in common: they took their football very seriously.

"So does the current Superior high school football coach, Tom Mestelle. Sometimes, Tom is tough on the media and very stern with his players, but he gets results. I'd say he's probably the best of the current high school coaches in our area.

"We've had some outstanding high school coaches right here in our neck of the woods: the late Cliff Thompson in Eveleth, for instance, who got high school hockey started in Northern Minnesota. Look at just a few of his former players: John Mayasich, Matchefts, Mariucci, Frank Brimsek, Connie Pleban, Sam LoPresti and former Golden Bears who went on to coaching, like Willard Ikola, that great Eveleth goalie, who's had a stellar career at Edina—the 'winningest high school hockey coach in Minnesota.' In the U.S. Hockey Hall of Fame at Eveleth, Cliff is surrounded by his own former players, and justly so. He and many of his players contributed so much to developing high school hockey and professionalism among young people in our state.

"In basketball, Duluth Central's Jim Hastings shines. When Jim took Central down to the state in 1967 it was the first time a high school team looked like a team, on and off the court. Jim personally led a drive to outfit the team in matching blazers and ties, and it did something for them. They looked like what they were: first-class young men, sharp kids, in the hotels and at the arena. Their conduct was exemplary, and I think those Trojan blazers gave them team pride. Jim not only taught kids basketball; he taught them how to live and act.

"Hastings was a taskmaster who left nothing to chance. He had those kids ready for anything. When they were supposed to take a shot from the edge of the key on a certain type of screen, they drilled that play in practice until it was second nature. When Hastings fielded a team, they were prepared, mentally and physically. They went to nine state tournaments and never lost a first-round game. He'd say, 'A lot of teams were just happy to get to the state. I'd try to get our kids to believe they belonged there and could actually win.'

"Another great prep coach was Harvey Isle, a Virginia boy whose career at Tower-Soudan was cut short by early death in August 1963. Strategy is a key element in the success of any coach—Grant, Selman, Sertich, Hastings, Ikola—and Harvey Isle, too. He'd sit on the bench and watch the game like a hawk. He'd analyze the opposing team, and his mind would process what he saw like a computer. As fast as something happened on the floor, he'd have the countermeasure for it, a kind of sixth sense. It might take the rest of us 'til next day to come up with a countermove. Harvey did it instantly. It was uncanny.

"Bob McDonald at Chisholm has made that city *the* basketball town in Minnesota. His dedication to kids and his integrity have made him a legend.

"Les Knuti at Esko also was in a class by himself. He'd have been an ideal choice for UMD athletic director years ago. He was an early area athletic promoter. He started a holiday basketball tournament, the Midway River Classic, that eventually was copied over the whole state because it allowed teams to play extra games during the season. He'd bring in eight teams and everybody had a ball. The highlight was the party he and his wife, Hildegard, would throw at their home.

"In one of his last years as football coach, Esko was way ahead, something like 55 to zip late in the fourth quarter. I don't remember who they were playing, but it was a disaster. As Esko lined up for a kickoff, I looked out at the field and thought to myself, 'Seems like a lot of people out there. Those guys are shoulder-to-shoulder across the 40-yard line.' Later, I kidded Knuti about it. He grinned and said, 'Yeah, Marsh, I had 17 men on the field on that play. Just wanted to see if the refs were awake, but nobody caught it!'"

Marsh leans forward to make a point.

"I have the utmost respect for all coaches. To coach, you have to have thick skin, whether you're in high school, college, the NFL, NHL, Big Ten. A coach gets very little credit, and a lot of unearned blame. If your team is winning, fans say it's because you had a good runner, a wizard of a quarterback, or a guy who can shoot baskets or goals from anywhere on the floor or ice. To the public, it's always the players who are responsible for winning. But if you have a losing team, most fans will blame the coach: he doesn't use the right plays, doesn't put in his best players, or call the right strategy. It's always the coach who loses, and the players who win."

A few officials stand out, too.

"I'll always remember Bill Selman at UMD. His relationships with referees and officials was one of mutual respect. I've heard him tell one of his players, 'You worry about playing right wing,

I'll worry about the officials. If you guys made as few mistakes as the officials, we'd be in the NCAA every year!'

"I don't think I have the courage to be a coach, and I'm *sure* I don't have the courage to be an official. I always made it a practice, when broadcasting sports, particularly hockey, not to criticize an official as long as he was hustling and in the proper position to make a call. The officials have a different perspective than we in the press box, a different view of the play than most fans in the stands. In some cases, they even see things differently from another official on the same ice, or same field or floor.

"I've had some favorites over the years. Hank Jensen, long-time pro at Enger Park golf course, is one of the dearest guys I know. My first contact with him was when he refereed college hockey and, as I've already mentioned, Macalester never got any calls our way when Hank was officiating. But he always called 'em the way he saw 'em. Hank always has been a champion of ways to make hockey a better and cleaner game.

"Steve Kersie of Gilbert has spent his life as a coach, athletic director and administrator. No one is more interested in high school athletics than 'Kers.'

"Jack Malevich of Eveleth was outstanding, and he had his own style, both as a football coach and a referee. He worked a lot of high school basketball games when I was playing in Tower-Soudan. Sometimes, it was a little embarassing when he'd call a foul. He didn't just raise his hand and blow the whistle. He'd explain that foul, and everybody in the gym would know what you did wrong. He'd come up to you and say, 'No. 9, you pushed that man,' or 'No. 10, you gave that man an elbow!' Jack was an excellent official, and he's a nice guy to top it off.

"The best officiated high school basketball game I ever saw was called by the late Jud Gregor from Nashwauk. When his partner didn't show up for a game between Tower-Soudan and Ely—two real rivals—Jud worked the game all alone and did an absolutely

142

magnificent job. I remember that—but I don't remember who won.

"Bob Gilray from the Canadian Soo was an outstanding hockey official. When Gilray got off the ice a couple of years, Burt Smith, one-time commissioner of the WCHA, appointed him as supervisor of officials, and Bob took WCHA officiating to a new high of professionalism. He'd take notes, write down the good and bad calls by his officials. After the game, he'd have a private 'prayer meeting' with the ones he thought had made bad decisions.

"Everett 'Buck' Riley and Stan Hegg of International Falls and Fort Frances worked as a team and handled most of the UMD hockey games in the 1960s. They drove to Duluth together and on that long trip from the border they would recite the hockey rule book to each other.

"I also consider it a great privilege to have known some of the best National Football League officials—men like the late Tommy Bell and Jim Tunney.

"When Tommy made an appearance at a high school athletic banquet in Silver Bay some years back, I had a rare opportunity to spend time with him, talking about the fine points of NFL play. I picked up some invaluable tips, most importantly the signals for penalties and when to look for them, as well as how to distinguish among the mannerisms of the various referees who used the same basic signals.

"Locally, I've always admired Don Wilkie of Duluth. Don's done a great job as a hockey referee. I don't think there's a hockey rule he doesn't know. I know he took a lot of heat from the fans when he worked UMD games. Really, I suppose he never should have been assigned to UMD games—he's from Duluth and he played for the Bulldogs. It must have been a real chore for Don to remain neutral—but he always did. In fact, he bent over backward so the other teams couldn't say he favored the home club. I don't think it's good to have a local man officiate a home game, particularly an alumnus. Yet, it happens all over the WCHA. Don Wilkie handles it very well, but he's the exception.

"There were always two referees for a hockey game in years gone by. Now, there's only one. I don't buy the idea that one man can handle a hockey game. Every other sport has increased the number of officials in recent years. Nearly every basketball game has three. The National Football League has seven men on the field, and one in the replay booth. Yet, what in the world have we done to hockey? We've gone from two officials down to one—in the fastest game on earth! It's a big mistake.

"In baseball, we started out with one umpire behind the plate, then it was a luxury to have a base umpire. First thing you know, we had a plate umpire and four base umpires, and now they've gone to six umpires—they've even got a foul line official in the majors.

"Then, there's Bruce Froemming, a great National League umpire who started in the minors, right here in Duluth with the old Northern League. I remember one incident when Bruce shut down a game because of some unsportsmanlike comments shouted from the press box. It was probably the only time in baseball history when an umpire ordered the press box cleared out before allowing the game to go on."

Bruce Bennett also recalls that game:

"I was reporting the game for the *News-Tribune*, and I was also the official scorer," Bennett says. "It was back in 1960, and the Dukes were playing the Winnipeg Goldeyes in historic Wade Stadium. Froemming was home plate umpire, and John Collins was first base umpire.

"Gates Brown of the Dukes hit a line drive to right field. It was a solid hit, and he tried for a double. The throw from the fielder went over the head of the shortstop, who was covering second base. Brown came into second and the shortstop faked a catch and made a phantom tag. The ball actually went to third.

"To Collins, the first base umpire, that phantom tag looked

pretty authentic, and he called an out. The crowd went wild. In the press box, we had a perfect view and it was pretty obvious that ball wasn't caught by the shortstop.

"Now in Wade, the sounds on the field carried clearly to the press box—even conversation. Unfortunately, it worked the other way just as well. In the box, we could hear most of the rhubarb on the field between the umpires and Dukes manager Frank Carswell. Frank had retrieved the ball near third and was forcefully explaining to Froemming: 'If the shortstop caught the ball, how come I've got it?'

"Marsh and some of the others in the box were shouting some well-chosen but not-too-delicately-phrased suggestions about the fine points of umpiring and, since the sound carried equally well in both directions, Froemming heard them.

"He overruled Collins' decision and called Brown safe at second. Then, he suspended play and ordered everybody out of the press box. That meant Marsh, Stan May of the *Superior Evening Telegram*, Dukes' business manager 'Soup' Stromme and Arno Goethel of the *News-Tribune*.

"I don't remember why Arno was there because, as sports editor at the time, he was my boss. Anyway, Froemming threatened to forfeit the game if the press box wasn't cleared immediately. Everybody started to leave—everybody, that is, except Goethel. He grabbed the phone and tried to call Northern League President Herman White in Eau Claire to complain. Arno was lying on the floor, out of sight, while he made the call.

"I left the box, went down to the field and reminded Froemming that I was the official scorer and, 'If you throw me out, you won't have an official game.' He relented and sent me back—but everybody else in the press box had to get out of the stadium. Finally, he allowed the game to proceed."

Stromme, the club's business manager, had to buy a general admission ticket to watch the rest of the game from the cheap seats.

The venerable Wade Stadium has had many glory moments. "It's one of the best stadiums of its size in the country," Marsh says.

"One of my most memorable moments at Wade was the day Bill Freehan made his debut with the Duluth Dukes. He'd just been signed from the University of Michigan's Wolverine baseball team where he'd been a real standout. It was his first time at the plate in pro ball. There was the crack of the bat as he lined a shot down the left field line for a double. The crowd roared, and I turned to the guy next to me and said, 'That's Bill Freehan? We're going to like him!'

"He didn't even finish the season with the Dukes before he was called up to the next classification by Detroit. He went on to a great career with the Tigers, but his first base hit as a pro was in Wade Stadium with the Duluth Dukes."

Marsh opens the kitchen door and steps out on the redwood deck overlooking the back yard. Below, Judy tends a rock garden of flowers. A few steps away is Marsh's own tiny plot of tilled soil, a postage-stamp size vegetable garden.

"I always helped with Dad's garden when I was a kid," he says. "It's a good way to stay humble."

He settles into a worn deck chair.

"I've really been very fortunate to have been allowed to spend my life doing what I love, associating with people I admire. I've been paid for doing what I'd be willing to do free. I'll never be rich, but I've had a ball, literally and figuratively. I feel sorry for people who are locked into work they don't like, or simply tolerate, five days a week.

"I've had the rare privilege of knowing and working with some truly fine broadcasters, writers, players, coaches, officials and the fans themselves. For the most part, the people I've worked for over the years, my bosses, have been tolerant, understanding, supportive.

"You're never free in this business. Nearly every aspect of my life has been programmed by time. Everything Judy and I do is dictated by the clock. I've missed some things other people have had because of that. If I'd worked from eight to five, I'd have been done for the day and could take my wife to dinner or to a movie, or go fishing, or just sit home and read or talk.

"I guess you can second-guess yourself 'til you're blue in the face. There have been frustrations but, on the other hand, too few to mention when you balance them against the good times. No, I don't have any regrets. There aren't many things I'd change, even if I could. I wonder how many people my age can honestly say that.

"I've always done the very best I can—and I'm grateful that it's been accepted as well as it has. I've always tried to be honest with people and say exactly what I think. I'd be telling a lie if I said I didn't want people to like me and accept me the way I am. I've been blessed with the respect of my friends and colleagues—and that's worth a lot, something money can't buy.

"It's been a thrill and an honor to be center stage for nearly 40 years, and I'm thankful for the privilege."

# Index of Names

# Gunflint:
## Reflections on the Trail
by Justine Kerfoot

Justine Kerfoot has lived on Minnesota's remote Gunflint trail for five decades. She's gutsy and knowledgeable and humorous, most of all she's real—a unique woman of strength and character! Her keen observations and warm sensitivity recreate memorable episodes and touching moments from her years on the trail.

This is Justine's second book. Her first book, *Woman of the Boundary Waters*, was an instant success.

Hardcover, 208 pages, $16.95
Illustrations by Nancy Hemstad
ISBN 0-938586-43-2

# Teaching Kids to Love the Earth
by Marina Lachecki Herman, Ann Schimpf, Joseph Passineau & Paul Treuer

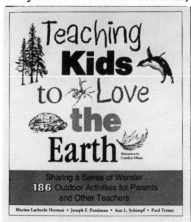

Softcover, 192 pages, $14.95
Illustrations by Carolyn Olson
ISBN 0-938586-42-4

*Teaching Kids to Love the Earth* is a collection of 186 earth-caring activities designed for use with children of all ages to help them experience and appreciate the earth.

This book leads you through the authors' Sense of Wonder Circle: curiosity, exploration, discovery, sharing and passion. Each chapter contains a story, instructions for a main activity, suggestions for related activities and a list of additional resources. *Teaching Kids to Love the Earth* will enable you and the children you work with to experience a "sense of wonder" about the world we share.

*"The authors are true to their word, **Teaching Kids to Love the Earth** gently and lovingly educates, excites and creates a sense of awe about the magic of our earth. This book needs to be in the hands of anyone who has or even knows a child."*

**David Emmerling, Ph.D, The National Wellness Institute, Inc.**

# Distant Fires by Scott Anderson

*"Distant Fires brought me back to the days of illustrating for Sig Olson and Calvin Rutstrum. It has the same charm as Sig and Calvin's writing and it has inspired me to begin illustrating again."*

**Les Kouba, wildlife artist**

Softcover, 180 pages,
Illustrations by Les Kouba   $12.95
ISBN 0-938586-33-5

Distant Fires is a classic canoe-trip story— with a twist of wry. Author Scott Anderson's journey was something more than just a portage-and-paddle adventure. Certainly it was the only such journey to begin on a front porch in Duluth, Minnesota, and end — three months and 1,700 miles later — at the historical York Factory on the shores of Hudson Bay. And with every turn of the page, author Scott Anderson treats the reader to a breath of fresh northwoods air.

Put two 22-year-olds in a canoe for a trek they've dreamed about all their lives, and you've got a guarantee for adventure . . . and misadventure. Put *Distant Fires* in your hands and you've got a delightful read.

*"Anyone with the slightest streak of adventure will understand the challenge and relish Anderson's telling."*

**-Booklist**

*"Eric Sevareid and Walter Port would be proud of **Distant Fires** and the young men who lived the adventure. So would the beloved stern paddle Sigurd Olson. Distant Fires belongs in your packsack, along with the maps and stuff that keep us all from losing our way."*

**George Vukelich, Wisconsin Public Radio**

*"Scott Anderson and his partner made the Minnesota-York Factory canoe voyage somewhat differently from the Port-Sevareid trip in 1930 and I think they did it more intelligently. But the physical, moral and, I might say, religious experience is much the same. Some of his phrasing is very happy indeed: 'the resting place of the rivers.' I wish I had written that."*

**Eric Sevareid, Consultant, CBS News**

# Best Book for Young Adults 1991
## Awarded by the American Library Association

# Bering Bridge: The Soviet-American Expedition from Siberia to Alaska by Paul Schurke

Twelve Soviet and American adventurers set out from Siberia in mid-winter 1989 on an epic journey across 1,000 miles of arctic tundra. This unprecedented trek was the first expedition since the advent of the Cold War to travel between the USA and the USSR across the Bering Strait.

Visiting native Siberian villages along their route, these dog sled diplomats helped build a bridge of friendship that now connects people of the Bering Strait region, and all citizens of the USA and the USSR.

More than just a dramatic adventure, *Bering Bridge* is a story of peace.

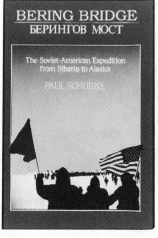

Hardcover, 240 pages photos
ISBN 0-938586-31-9    $17.95

# Wilderness Daydreams

Escape to the wilderness — no matter where you are! Naturalist Douglas Wood serves as a guide for your personal wilderness journey. Relax and enjoy the sounds and images of nature as Doug's gentle voice leads you to places of solitude, peace and renewal. With original guitar music and environmental sounds.

**Wilderness Daydreams 1: Canoe/Rain**

Side A: Canoe trip with gentle guitar accompaniment. (23 min)
Side B: Safe haven in the rain with background sounds of the storm. (23 min)
Audio cassette/$9.95

**Wilderness Daydreams 2: Island/Spring**

Side A: Island trek with soothing classical guitar accompaniment. (23 min)
Side B: Sunny spring day with authentic sounds of the marsh. (23 min)
Audio cassette/$9.95

**Wilderness Daydreams 3: Campfire/Stream**

Side A: Gaze into the campfire lulled by a quiet guitar. (23 min)
Side B: Explore a forest stream with sounds of nature all around. (23 min)
Audio cassette/$9.95

# Up North

by Sam Cook

In this memorable collection of essays and stories, columnist Sam Cook portrays the enchanting North Country that is as much a state of mind as a geographical area. These stories are more than mere tales of hunting and fishing, paddling and portaging. They are journeys into the soul. In his witty, touching style, Sam Cook offers insights about life set against the backdrop of the North Country's magic.

Hardcover, 192 pages, $16.95
ISBN 0-938586-09-2

# Quiet Magic

by Sam Cook

In his second book Sam Cook scores again with another delightful collection of essays and stories from the North Country. Readers are treated to powerful imagery, gentle humor and keen insights in richly evocative stories of the outdoors: rugged fishing trips, conversation before the next day's hunt, an "ugly campsite" that becomes a home for two, and the winter's mid-winter slumber in a snow house for one.

Hardcover, 192 pages, $16.95
ISBN 0-938586-17-3

Sam Cook trekked north from his native Kansas in 1976 to work for an outfitter in the Superior-Quetico canoe country. Now he uses Duluth, Minnesota, as "base camp" for his warm, insightful outdoors columns for the Duluth News-Tribune.

*"An uncommonly compassionate writer, Cook is arguably Minnesota's best-loved newspaper columnist . . . "*

**William Souder, Minnesota Monthly**

*"Sam can bring memories of a blizzard into your living room with such remembrance that even though you may be sitting in front of a roaring fire you will feel the bite of the snow upon your face. Sam is good!"*

**Wally Pease, The Outdoor Press, Washington State**

# Order Form

Pfeifer Hamilton Publishers        800-247-6789 TOLL FREE
1702 E Jefferson Street                218-728-6807
Duluth, MN 55812-2029              218-728-2631 FAX

> Quantity discounts are available for retail distribution,
> executive gifts and incentive programs.

**SHIP THE FOLLOWING**

| Quantity | Title | Price | Total |
|---|---|---|---|
| _____ | Marsh: A Lifetime in Sports | 12.95 | _____ |
| _____ | Gunflint: Reflections on the Trail | 16.95 | _____ |
| _____ | Teaching Kids to Love the Earth | 14.95 | _____ |
| _____ | Distant Fires | 12.95 | _____ |
| _____ | Bering Bridge | 17.95 | _____ |
| _____ | Quiet Magic | 16.95 | _____ |
| _____ | Up North | 16.95 | _____ |
| _____ | Wilderness Daydreams 1 | 9.95 | _____ |
| _____ | Wilderness Daydreams 2 | 9.95 | _____ |
| _____ | Wilderness Daydreams 3 | 9.95 | _____ |

|  |  |
|---|---|
| Item Total | _____ |
| (Minnesota residents add 6% tax) |  |
| (Duluth residents add 7% tax) | _____ |
| Shipping | $3.00 |
| TOTAL ENCLOSED | _____ |

**PAYMENT METHOD**

_____ Check enclosed payable to Pfeifer-Hamilton

Bill my: _____ VISA _____ Master Card

# _____ - _____ - _____ - _____ Expires _____

Signature: _____

Name _____

Address _____

City/State/ZIP _____

Daytime Phone ( _____ ) _____